STELLAKIS STYLIANOU
WITH DAVID HANCOCK

S✝ILKS

THE TRUE STORY OF THE HARDEST
BOUNCER IN BRITAIN

JOHN BLAKE

Published by John Blake Publishing Ltd, 3 Bramber Court,
2 Bramber Road, London W14 9PB, England

First published in hardback in 2002

ISBN 1 903402 95 6

British Library Cataloguing-in-Publication Data: A catalogue record
for this book is available from the British Library.

Typeset by GDADesign

Printed and bound in Great Britain by CPD (Wales)

1 3 5 7 9 10 8 6 4 2

Papers used by John Blake Publishing Ltd are natural, recyclable products
made from wood grown in sustainable forests. The manufacturing processes
conform to the environmental regulations of the country of origin.

Every attempt has been made to contact the relevant copyright-holders, but
some were unobtainable. We would be grateful if the appropriate people could
contact us.

C⊕NTENTS

DEDICATION

I WOULD LIKE TO DEDICATE THIS BOOK TO MY WIFE SHEENA FOR PUTTING UP WITH ME FOR THE LAST TWENTY-TWO YEARS ON THE DOOR.

INTRODUCTION

TIMES HAVE CHANGED. AUTHORITY HAS FOUND MORE AND MORE WAYS OF MAKING PEOPLE CONFORM AND LEAD 'NORMAL' LIVES.

Stellakis Stylianou, or 'Stilks' to people he likes – and dislikes – is quite unique in his chosen lifestyle. He has achieved status and standing by not conforming.

This is not a gangland story *per se*, neither is it a story of underworld skullduggery, but a true account of a remarkable character with an ability to see clearly, act fairly, and be prepared to show extreme violence where necessary.

You will not come into contact with this man unless you move in his world, so you will not benefit from his wisdom and philosophy. Neither can you know what it means to face his fearsome tone and manner.

But here's your chance. How many times have you been

taken advantage of, or felt intimidated, or felt that you are not being listened to?

Stilks says, 'It's not because you haven't expressed yourself, but rather you haven't made them fear you enough. Fear gets respect, remember that.'

Now meet the head doorman face to face.

Tony Papa-Adams

PROLOGUE

THERE'S SOMETHING ABOUT BEING TOUGHENED – OK, 'HARD', IF YOU LIKE – THAT GIVES YOU A SECOND SENSE ABOUT WHEN IT'S GONNA GO OFF. YOU CAN SMELL IT; YOU CAN FEEL IT. IT'S IN THE AIR. IT'S EVERYWHERE. YEARS OF KNOWING IT; LOOKIN' AT THE PUNTERS; SIZIN' 'EM UP. YOU JUST KNOW WHO'S TROUBLE AND WHERE IT'S LIKELY TO COME FROM. AND THEN ONE DAY, ALL OF A SUDDEN, IT HAPPENS RIGHT OUT OF THE BLUE ... AND YOU AIN'T EXPECTING IT. IT HAPPENED TO ME WHEN I WAS GOING DOWN THE KEBAB SHOP. I LOOKED AROUND AND SUDDENLY REALISED I MIGHT HAVE BITTEN OFF A BIT MORE THAN I COULD CHEW.

This night-stick hit me on the back of my left shoulder – *wallop*! There were four of the fuckers. I thought, Bollocks, this ain't fair. I noticed the sticks, the pick-axe handles first. And the funniest thing is, there was no fear. You don't have any time to be afraid. I thought, Right, move in fast. Up close it's impossible for them to get any swing on the clubs. And I was up there, I was in the middle of it. I was fighting for my life, as I've always fought …

I'd been on the door down at the Station Hotel in Welling, South London. I think it's called The Moon and Sixpence or something poncey now. Back then, in the Eighties, it was the first Whitbread venue pub that had bouncers on the door. And this particular night it was packed with the usual bunch of drinkers, some rowdy, some laughing, most pissed, place heaving. And there were these Millwall supporters. They looked like trouble and I wasn't surprised when the buzzer went at the pub entrance to tell us guys on the door that something was going off inside. I rushed in, flexed up, ready.

The hooligans had been jostling the crowd, spilling drinks and generally looking for trouble. We steamed in. I recognised the leader, he had a reputation for being the hardest of the Millwall supporters and he had a team of about half-a-dozen other scum with him. They had already smashed the place up once before and ruined a day down there when Brian Jacks and Henry Cooper had made a special charity appearance. That was the sort of little bastards they were.

Anyway, they weren't gonna do it again. There were four of us on that night, so we grabbed hold of 'em. They tried to be a bit cocky and I said, 'Listen, I ain't interested in what you got to say, you been causing trouble in here long enough. Now you're out – fuck off.'

They struggled a little bit but it didn't take much to restrain 'em. There were a few verbals on the door, the usual old thing with the main bloke mouthing off, 'I'll be back to shoot ya', and all that old bollocks. I've heard it a hundred times. To most of 'em, I just say, 'Don't jump the queue!' As far as I was concerned that was the end of the incident and they were barred for life. But there was a surprise in store.

At the end of the night, we emptied the place and I told the other lads I was off down the road to get meself a kebab and I'd be back. So I'm walking down the road and I see four or five blokes over on the opposite side but don't think anything of it. Then I twig it's the scum I threw out of the pub an hour or so earlier, but I figure they ain't gonna do anything because here we were in the middle of Bellegrove Road in Welling, a major bloody road … How wrong can you get?

First, I hear the screaming as they charge towards me. I couldn't run back to the Station so I decided to run towards 'em. That's when the first one clobbered me with the pick-axe handle or whatever it was. That made me mad. Another one tried to have a go but I was too close in by then and I blocked it.

I grabbed that one and pulled him down to the floor; he was gonna be the first one I was putting out the way. I'd got my hand on his face and was twisting it when – *squelch*! – I realised I'd got my fingers in one eye so I decided to push 'em right into the sockets. He was screaming, squealing like a pig as I pushed harder trying to flip his fucking eyeball out.

With that, the others surrounded me and started clubbing me over the back with planks of wood and then smashing me over the head with the pick-axe handles. I was thinking, I don't give two shits … I'm gonna do this one I've got on the floor before they do me. If I was gonna go unconscious, I wanted at least one of 'em out of the way so I'd got some sort of revenge.

The blows continued raining down on me but I didn't give a shit; I was flattening the guy on the floor mercilessly. He wasn't gonna look a pretty sight – if he survived at all. Then, all of a sudden, I hear this sound of a car horn and look up to recognise one of the other bouncers, Dave Kilroy, racing down the road full tilt. And I thought, Fuck, he ain't gonna stop! So I managed to stand up and grab the bloke I'd been pounding off the floor and, with barely a second to spare, I jumped out of the way of Dave's car. But the other guy wasn't so lucky and Dave hit him and sprayed him across the bonnet. He went straight over the car and rolled back down into the road. He was out cold. One down, three to go. I still thank Dave regularly for saving my life.

By this time, the other doormen were on their way and I knew we'd be squaring up for a good one. I'd taken a lot of blows but this was the job I'd trained for. I could take a few hits and, anyway, you don't feel any pain 'cos the adrenalin has kicked in and by then I was fucking mad. So I grab one of the bastards with the sticks and just then one of the other doormen hits him as hard as he can. Even I felt it. He went down like a building being demolished. Even in the middle of all this, I had to give my mate a wink as if to say, 'Where the fuck did you pull that one from?' So I started kicking the bloke who was on the floor while the other two scum ran off into the bushes.

Remember, these blokes had been trying to kill me and I was gonna teach 'em the biggest fuckin' lesson of their lives. This wasn't half-hearted – blood was streaming from my head, I was covered in lumps, they weren't playing with me and I wasn't playing with them either. I looked a complete mess, my dinner jacket ripped to shreds, bow-tie torn off. But I had one little surprise for the guy on the floor. I said to him, 'Are you all right, mate?' And he must of thought the ruckus had come to an end, so he dropped his guard and, as he pulled his hands away from his face, I stamped on his head.

'My name's *Stilks*,' I said. And then I stamped again. '*Stilks*.' Another stamp. '*Stilks*.' Another. 'And don't you ever fucking forget it!'

1

WHEN THE GOING GETS TOUGH

**IF YOU CHASE TWO RABBITS
YOU WON'T CATCH EITHER**

STILKS

THE INCESSANT, RHYTHMIC WHIRR OF AN OLD SEWING MACHINE WAS THE SOUND OF MY CHILDHOOD.

It was always there in the background as my mum sewed together anything for the East End sweat shops that paid her a pittance and kept our whole family in a state of poverty. At times, we barely knew where the next meal was coming from and, as for luxuries like a television or toys to play with, forget it. Those sort of things were for other people, not for us.

The only time the sewing machine stopped was so my mum could cook us dinner.

My mum and dad, Helene and Andreas Stylianou, had come to Britain from Cyprus after the war, hoping to build a better future for themselves. They were grafters, Dad working in a butter factory on the production line turning out pack after pack of the stuff, while Mum was at her sewing machine all hours that God sent.

I came along on 21 July 1958. Stellakis Stylianou, after me grandad. But why don't you just call me Stilks. Everyone else does.

I'm told I was born in London University Hospital, within one mile of Bow Bells, which makes me a cockney, but I can't remember the very early years. For me, home was in Plumstead, South London, a little three-bedroom Victorian terraced house in Wickham Lane, where you could hear everything that went on because all we had was bare floorboards and old pieces of lino. The place would fairly echo. There was an outside toilet and a boiler in the kitchen which we stoked up with coal to get hot water. Hot water was scarce so we all had to use the same water when we had a bath, which was a tin one in the kitchen.

And the sound of that sewing machine would drone on all the time.

We might have had fuck all, but we were a close-knit family and, when my sister Yianoula was born two years after me and my baby sister Maria a couple of years later, the family seemed to be complete. The only thing was, none of us spoke English. At home with the family and with our friends, we all spoke Greek. In fact, I didn't learn English 'til I went to Galleon's Mount Infants School at the age of seven. And I hated it at the beginning, 'cos I didn't know anyone and I couldn't speak the lingo. And it was only when I was sitting at my desk, looking pained and

4

crossing my legs, that I had the courage to stick my hand up in the air.

'Toilet?' said Miss, pointing her questioning finger at me.

And that was the first word I ever learned in the English language – 'Toilet'.

After a few days I got settled into school and one of my first friends was Mark Rowe, who now promotes Julius Francis, the boxer. Even in those days, we used to pretend to be karate experts going round the playground trying to chop up pieces of wood with our bare hands. The only result of that was that I was always going home with bruised hands. But I was never questioned by my parents 'cos they were always working and we didn't get that much time with 'em.

But the wonderful thing about my childhood is that we had these massive woods right behind the house, and that became the place to play. We'd march all around, roll over, jump up, laugh and become lost in them. It was in the woods that I found this rusty old bicycle frame. I knew what it was. I had wanted a bicycle for so long, I'd cried in front of Dad for one. That's how desperate it got.

Anyway, with the frame well stored I went in search of the wheels. My mate Keith Waghorn got me one and I forget where the other one came from, but anyway, we got 'em. The gears and chain were a piece of piss, and I was off. I kept the bike in me den in the woods. And I got it ready for the day of me birthday – 21 July. Mum and Dad had bought me a pair of shoes! So I snuck away in the afternoon and got my bike out. I was ready to ride ... And it was all going fine 'til

I started to have a race with Keith going down Gravel Hill. I was doing about 30mph when I realised we hadn't fitted any brakes. I thought, Shit. The only way to stop myself was by putting me feet on the road. And I had to do this from about three-quarters of the way down 'cos there was a crossroads at the bottom. And that was it, sparks on the tarmac, soles burning up. I stopped just before the major road junction, and fell off …

When my mum saw me shoes she went fucking ballistic. They were ruined. I'd only get a pair of shoes once a year and I had to look after them, but these were fucking ruined. Dad comes running in, spots the shoes, and then I know I'm in for a beating. My dad was a big fella, 6ft tall, 19st, he only had to hit you once and you knew it. And I'll tell you what, I've taken a few beatings in my time but the one that left a real impression was the one I got from my dad when I ruined me new shoes.

I was always getting into scrapes, mainly 'cos we had to amuse ourselves all the time. We didn't even have a fucking telly until I was eight years old and then it was one of them that kept going wonky and you had to hit it on the side.

I was a cheeky bugger and I remember one day thinking, How can I annoy Mum? My sister Maria was only four at the time. There was a ladder me dad left out at the back of the house where he had been painting the windows. So I made Maria climb to the top of this ladder and stand on the ledge, then I went and told me mum, 'Look, Mum, Maria's climbed up the ladder and she's stuck on the second-floor ledge.'

Mum went mad, but she thought of the kids first all the time so she had to try and climb this ladder herself. There she was swaying about and I was pissing myself laughing. Us kids were always pulling as many tricks on each other as we could. You see, we were bored most of the time.

When I was about eight or nine, me and a couple of other kids in the gang used to go round to these greenhouses where they grew tomatoes. And we'd throw stones at the greenhouses and break the glass. We had no intention of nicking the tomatoes or anything like that. We used to like breaking the windows and listening to the glass smashing. Then I'd go round the front and I'd tell the bloke I'd seen these boys throwing stones. I'm sure the bloke could see through it, but he would give me a bit of change to make sure the kids didn't do it any more. Remember, we didn't have any money for sweets and stuff and that was the way I'd make a bit.

When I did get up to mischief, I think it was because I kept having to prove meself. You see, I was a really sickly child. I know if you look at me now, 16st and a threat to the unruly, then you won't believe it. But I'm telling ya, I was a weak kid; I couldn't have been more than 6st, I was always in and out of hospital. I suffered from acute mastoiditis or something, which affects one of the bones in your ear. So I was always having operations on my ear. Me grandmother and me dad had bad ears, so from birth I was always having earaches and I was always ill. If it weren't me ear, it was me appendix.

I can still smell the wards and corridors of St Nicholas Hospital, Plumstead. They would echo and smell of Dettol. I can remember going in there, having me ear done, going home for a week and then going back for another operation. Mastoiditis is when the bone in the ear goes off and it seeps smelly pus out of your ear. So they have to cut away the bone; it's a two-hour operation. If they don't do it right, your face can drop and it can affect your brain as well. I had loads of operations but they never put it right on the National Health. It was only about eight years ago when I went and had it done privately that it was put right. Bloody National Health Service.

I'd be happy to get home from hospital. There was something reassuring about the background noise in our house.

The first weapon I ever had, if you can call it that, was a bow and arrow I made up in the woods. I was really proud of it and after I'd done all the target practice at the trees, I thought, What can I shoot now? And there was me sister. It was a pure accident but I shot her in the head. Here was this big, long stick lodged in her head and she was screaming and crying. Me mum had to take her up the hospital to have this arrow removed. So there we was again up the bloody St Nicholas.

Some nurses said, 'Hello, Mrs Stylianou, and what's the matter now?'

What's the matter now – was she fucking blind? Here was a small child with an arrow sticking out of its head.

'My sister's got a headache,' I said cheekily, which earned a clip round the ear from Mum. That hospital's been closed down now and I'm not surprised; once our family stopped going, there probably wasn't much reason to keep it open.

But I felt really bad about what I'd done to our Maria, even though Mum and Dad accepted it was an accident. And I got off lightly. But even to this day, I think it's one of the things that put me off using weapons when I got older. I use judo holds and me fists now and I've never injured another fucker by accident. If they got hurt, it was because they had it coming to 'em.

But in those days, when you're a kid, weapons are exciting and one day Dad came home with an air rifle. Dunno where he got it. Could have been from a mate at work or he could have got it out of a second-hand shop, which is where a lot of our stuff came from. Anyway, I thought, this is fucking brilliant. So I says, 'Dad, got any targets?'

He goes, 'Stellakis, this is not for target practice. I want you to go up in the woods and shoot pigeons so we can have something to eat! We're gonna have *pellafi*.'

'What the fuck's *pellafi*, Dad?'

'It's a Greek rice dish with pigeons.'

We were so poor now we were having to go hunting for our food in the middle of South London. So I started practising a bit to get me eye in and within a couple of days I was over the back. When you shoot pigeons out of the nest, you have to make sure the baby pigeons have grown to a good enough, edible size, but not so big that they can fly away. Shoot the mother first, then climb up the tree and you've got two more. Now ya got a meal.

Me dad showed me how to pluck the feathers and with the babies you'd pull their heads off. Just hold it and twist. I didn't like the idea at first, I thought it was cruel and that, but soon got the hang of it. I was soon eating everything – the sparrows, the blackbirds, the thrushes. Anything, as long as it wasn't a bird that eats meat. If a bird eats meat, like a crow, you can't eat it. But if it eats seed, you're alright.

By the age of 12, I was skinning a rabbit quite easily; just cut it round the throat, grab the skin and pull it and it comes off in one go like a jumper.

Our food was very basic. I remember coming home one night and me mum's at the sink and I've looked over and she's got this lamb's head. She was washing it and brushing the teeth.

'What ya doing, Mum?' I ask. 'Whassat?'

She says, 'It's a lamb's head.'

'But what are you brushing its teeth for?'

'Because we are going to eat it. You wait and see, it's nice.'

I knew proper joints of meat were expensive. But I thought, Nah, we're not gonna eat that, are we? So there was Mum cleaning it out; she pulls the tongue out and scrapes it, getting all the hairs and muck off it, washing it, preparing it. Then this head goes in the oven, with potatoes round it.

It comes out the oven and I can remember there was me and me two sisters, but only two eyes. So I goes, 'Dad, I'm havin' one of them.'

And he says, 'All right,' 'cos the son in Greek Cypriot families always gets the first choice of everything. So I put my finger in and pulled it out and the eye had all grown from being small in the socket to the size of a fucking golf ball. Dad said, 'Just put it in your mouth and suck,' and I can remember it just melted in me mouth. But there's a hard white bit left and you just spit that out.

There's a saying that the meat nearest the bone is the sweetest and the meat on the cheekbone of the lamb's head was a different class, it was really nice.

Then Dad got a hammer and he hit the lamb's head, cracking open the skull and removing the brain which he got out in one go with a spoon. He told me to eat it with salt and lemon and it would give me brains, too. Well, it never helped!

We used to eat really weird stuff. For years, I used to eat this stuff which I thought was liver until, one day, I asked someone if they had any 'soft liver' like me mum made. They said there was no such thing, so I asked Mum.

I said, 'You know that soft liver you give us …'

She stopped me right there and said, 'Son, that weren't no soft liver, that's the lungs.' I mean, honestly, the fucking lungs!

But our parents were the salt of the earth. They would scrimp and save and that sound that kept haunting me, that whirring drone of the sewing machine, was the sound of a working-class family trying to keep up and do their best.

I only remember ever having two holidays when I was a kid. One was to Margate and all I can remember then was going round the amusement arcade putting old pennies in the slot machines. And the other one, the big one, was when we all went to Cyprus.

Dad had announced we were going to Cyprus months and months before it happened. And I swear to God that bloody sewing machine went into overdrive. It was do-doing and der-dering it's little heart out right round the clock to try and get us the fares. There weren't many luxuries in our lives but now there were to be none at all; everything was being sacrificed to get us to Cyprus.

Even from a very small child, I'd dreamed of going there because Dad went on about it so much. How it was hot and sunny and not cold and damp like South London. But if I was cheeky enough to ask why he had left in the first place, it would be another fucking clip round the ear.

So me and me sisters were counting the days 'til we could go on our holiday to Cyprus. We'd never been anywhere exciting like that and we'd certainly never ever been in an aeroplane. It was all a bit too much for us to grasp. I was about ten at the time, I suppose, and I only realised we were really going on holiday when Mum bought me a new pair of swimming trunks. They were incredible ... bright red they were.

We went for two weeks and we was staying at my grandad's house in Nicosia, and we'd travel to the nearest beaches like Larnaca for days out or up to the Trodos mountains. There was something every day. One day, I remember, we found ourselves – me and me sisters – on the beach playing around and we decided to go in the sea. But 'cos of the mastoiditis I suffered from, I wasn't allowed to get me ear wet so just had to paddle around in the shallow bit by the beach. That was all right but it was boring, and so I started walking out a bit when all of a sudden the seabed dropped away … 'Cos I'd never been able to get me ear wet, I'd never been able to swim. I was still a paddler!

Suddenly I was bobbing around. I was going under and then twisting around and coming back up. There seemed to be a tremendous amount of water and it was dragging me away and dragging me down. They say your life flashes before you when you're drowning, and that's what happened to me. It hadn't been much of a poxy life. I was only ten years old and I'd spent it in South London. But it was the only one I'd had, and it was flashing before me. The thing was, I liked the feeling. If I could have that feelin' again I would. It's like this big *whoosh*, and everything you've done, you see it all again in seconds. It was an incredible experience … but I knew I was in real deep shit.

I was shouting for help, but Mum and Dad weren't on the beach, they must have gone for a cup of tea or something. There were only my two sisters. But the eldest one, Yianoula, who was only eight years old, came running into the sea. I thought, Fuck, she can't swim very well herself! She got to me, but with me panicking at the time, I pushed her down. And now there were both of us drowning. I remember I'd swallowed a lot of water and I was right at drowning point, lashing out, shouting, pushing Yianoula under. These sounds were in my head and I swear to this day it was that bloody sound of the sewing machine. It had haunted me throughout my little life and now it was gonna haunt me as I died.

I learned later that my little sister Maria had run up the beach to try and get some help. But I didn't know that and I couldn't cling on any longer. The sound was running through my head as the waves were washing over me and I was slowly slipping unconscious into the depths of the sea.

The last thing I remember was thinking, Mum's going be right fucking mad at me for drowning with me new swimming trunks on.

* * *

I wasn't surprised when I failed the 11+ exams, because I couldn't read or write. But I was surprised when I arrived at Bloomfield Secondary School in Plum Lane, Shooter's Hill. There were all these other kids and they were bigger than me!

The first time I was picked on it was just shoutin' names. They'd point at me and shout 'Rumple-STILKS-kin'. I'd been nicknamed Stilks at junior school, because who the fuck can remember Stellakis Stylianou! But the name had followed me to secondary school. I thought, Shit, I'm stuck with it for life now.

It was an old Victorian school. In fact, it was that old that when I got to the fifth year they built a new school, a right concrete jungle, called Eaglesfield, and closed Bloomfield down.

But when I first arrived at Bloomfield, it was very scary. Remember, I was still weedy and couldn't stand up for meself. Had no confidence, thought everyone was better than me. And so it was proved when I was streamed into the lowest class. And if you think it couldn't get any worse, it did, 'cos I managed to come bottom of that class. I was the idiot, the kid who couldn't read or write, the one they could pick on, bully and abuse. It was only later I discovered I was bloody dyslexic, or however you spell it. I'd do 'b' as 'd', 'p' as '9', '6' as 'b' and mix all the numbers up with the letters. I'd be physically sick if I had to do readin' or writin'. That just wasn't for me. Maths was the only thing I was any good at. It didn't take me long to catch on to equations.

Ping – the rubber band came hurtling at me and hit me on me ear. Me fucking mastoid ear! I looked round; there was sniggerin'. After that came the assault with the 12 in plastic rulers; if you flicked the end up, then it come down with a bigger force – on the back of my hand. It stung. Things weren't made any better by me mum, bless her, who insisted my uniform was always clean and my shirts perfectly ironed. The other kids must have thought I was stuck up, you know, a bit of a ponce. And, anyway, then disaster struck – I came top of the class. It was a total fluke – but nobody likes the number one bloke! I was in for it.

There was a group of about half-a-dozen boys, with this ringleader named Steve. He was a bit podgy but the tallest of 'em and, when you're growing up, height is the one thing that matters. Soon as the bloody teacher was out of the room, they'd pick on me. It was a case of, 'C'mon, let's go and beat Stilksy up.' They'd rush me. *Bang*! – in went a satchel; *whack*! – down came a ruler; *slap*! – that was the back of me head.

Then the teacher would come back and they'd jump into their seats. I used to dread the teacher leaving the room 'cos then I knew I was in for it. I got my share.

Maybe 'cos I was new to the class, or I didn't want to fight back – dunno, really – but I was the guy that got it. I think it's because I never liked to join in any team sports on account of my ill health, so I was never really a part of a gang. I was more of a loner. Even now I don't like team sports. I think real sport is on a one-on-one basis and, whenever the odds have been that, I rarely, if ever, lose. If you can't win on your own, I'm not interested in playing. The bullyin' would continue in the playground – maybe ten of 'em would come at me, taking me by surprise.

I can remember one day there was just me, the ringleader Steve and a mate of his, Steven, in this classroom. By now I was fucked off with being picked on, so for the first time I hit back. I clobbered this mate of Steve's and he went right over. I dunno who was more shocked, him or me. And then there was like another voice coming out me mouth and I said to Steve, 'And one day I'm gonna come back and do you as well.'

He laughed and said, 'You're fucking mad, Stilks. You'll never do me. Even when I've got a walking stick, I'll be doing you.'

I didn't think any more about it and went back to me weedy ways until I was about 14 years old when you had to decide what subjects you wanted to take and what sports you wanted to play.

'All those that want to do football over there,' barked the teacher. 'All those for tennis over there,' he pointed. 'All those for rugby, there.'

I was sitting down taking no notice. I was trying to do what I'd done for years, blend in and then bunk off 'cos it was Thursday afternoon sports period.

'Stylianou.'

'Sir.'

'Stylianou, what sport are you going to do?'

'Nothing, sir, I'm not well enough.'

'You've got to do a sport this year, Stylianou, you've got away with it long enough.'

'Football then, sir.'

'Football's taken.'

'Rugby, sir.'

'Rugby's taken.'

'What am I gonna do then, sir? I can't do swimming because I can't get water in me ear.'

'You're going to do judo, Stylianou. It'll make a man of you.'

So I look over to see who was going to be doing judo and thought, Fuck me … nah … fuck me! – it was bloody Steve and all his bullying mates. They'd all wanted to do the fighting sport.

So I says, 'No, sir, I don't want to do judo, it's not for me.'

'You get over there, Stylianou. That's what you are doing.'

I thought, Oh my God.

The judo lessons were given at Woolwich College in South London and the instructor was a fella called John Cole who is married to the sister of Brian Jacks, the Olympic judo medal winner. There was lots of sneering and taunting from Steve and his mob but John kept a tight rein on everything and there was fucking little they could do. But as soon as the lesson was over, I scarpered out of there first, in case any of 'em were trying to lay an ambush for me outside.

One week passed, two … three … four … and I was learning me holds and me throws. I was actually starting to bloody well enjoy it. Here was something at school I realised I liked doing. Then, one day, John said for the last ten minutes of the lesson we were all to practise with a partner. Of course, Muggins here got one of the bullies to partner. So I thought, Right, this is it. And lo-and-bloody-behold, the first thing I did was get him into a throw and bounce him down on the canvas. I was pushing him, pulling him, getting him in a hold … and a smile suddenly crossed my face. Fuck me, I thought, this kid isn't as good and brave as he thinks he is.

The following week, the same thing happened. OK, they were throwing me as well, but I was dishing out as much as I was taking, even more most times. I was beating 'em. I'd started putting on weight a bit, but more importantly I was gaining confidence, I was starting to believe in meself for the first time my life.

Then, one day, we were in woodwork class and the chief bully Steve tells me to go and get something for him. He was always ordering people around, the nasty piece of shit. I said, 'I ain't gonna go and do nothing for ya. Fuck off.'

So he's got a knife, and he's come over, and he's tried to stab me with the knife. So I grab his hand and start twisting it. But as I'm twisting it, hoping to hear it crack, the knife blade slashes across me … and he cuts me at the wrist. I manage to push him off and then says, 'Right, after lesson I'll see you outside.' I was sounding like a cartoon character. One minute I was mild-mannered Stellakis Stylianou, and the next I was fucking Super Stilks.

It seemed all the class and their mates had gathered to see what happened in the playground. Strangely, the only one who seemed apprehensive was Steve himself. He was holding back while I went straight into the ring, me wrist strapped up with an old bit of bandage. I thought, Fuck it, and immediately took the fight to Steve. I grabbed him by his shirt, pushed, pulled and twisted him like we'd been taught, heard his shirt rip, then got him into a neat hold and threw him on the floor. I started picking him up to give him a bit more when I thought, He ain't fucking worth it. So I threw him back on the floor, and that's when I heard his head crack.

'Don't try messing with me ever again,' I said. 'And don't forget to tell your mum how you got your fucking shirt torn.'

Now that I realised I could retaliate against anyone who threatened me, it must have gone to me head because I started to get unruly. I remember having the cane six times in one week. My judo was progressing, I was getting stronger and I was getting more and more into trouble. I became a nuisance; one of the kids disrupting the class all the time. I couldn't hear much because of the mastoiditis, so

I would sit at the back of the class and play up, doing me own thing and day-dreaming. In the end, the teachers started throwing me out of the classes until I was only allowed to take four subjects – Metalwork and Woodwork because I enjoyed 'em, and English and Maths 'cos I had to.

My Metalwork teacher was Terry Kilroy, who was head doorman at the Henry Cooper pub in the Old Kent Road and he would tell me these stories about his work as a bouncer which started to fire my imagination. He was also a British champion wrestler, so I'd always turn up at his class. But the other teachers didn't want to know me. And I can't fucking say I blame 'em.

With fuck all to do most of the day, I decided to set up a card school playing three-card brag. I'd find an empty classroom, get some of the other kids and we'd lock ourselves in. There were always about half-a-dozen of us and we'd play for money. Of course, I was still going home back to Wickham Lane where we lived as if I had been having a normal day at school, not gambling and beating people up. Mum kept on making sure my clothes were clean and fresh and tidy, so I suppose it came as a bit of a shock to my parents when I left school at 16 with no qualifications and I still couldn't read or write.

'Stellakis, doin' all this judo and weight training ain't gonna feed you,' my dad would shout at me. 'You've got to learn to read and write or when you're older you're gonna be banging your head against the wall. Sort your life out.' He always went on like that, but I wasn't listening.

When I wasn't doin' me sport, I was out nicking lead and copper wire from old houses and selling it. But Dad was worried about me and managed to get me an apprenticeship in Clerkenwell in London, near the City. It was nothing much. It was called McLauglin's Machinery who made presses for the printers.

It didn't last long, though. One day I saw these blokes humping this bloody machine outside.

The manager says to me, 'Stilks, get out there and help 'em.'

I said, 'It's raining. I ain't going out there. You go out in the rain.'

'You go out there now or you'll be sacked'

'I tell you what – I'm fucking off home.'

And that was the end of me apprenticeship.

The next day, a letter arrived from the firm addressed to me dad. It said I was useless to the company, useless to meself and useless to anyone.

So I went on the dole with me mate Keith and with our first week's dole money we bought a box of socks and we used to stand outside London Bridge. ''Ere ya go, six pairs for a pound, one for every day of the week – don't care what you get up to on a Sunday!' And then in the summer we'd knock out sunglasses, and that's what we did for money.

Judo was my big love and I was taking extra lessons in the evenings; Tuesdays and Thursdays. I was rising up the ranks, as they say. That's when I met Mick van Wyck. He was in the corner doing some curling with weights and told me it would improve me judo. And that fella later turned out to be Wolf from the *Gladiators*. But when I wasn't practising, I used to hang out at St Peter's Youth Club in Woolwich. I was always getting into trouble there and getting into fights. They used to have this pool table and people would put their money on the side for their turn next. I just used to walk by and scoop up the money and put it in me pocket.

One day, I was up to me tricks when this weird-looking guy came up to me and said, 'Hey, what you doing taking my money?'

Now most people wouldn't cause any fuss because me and my mate Mick 'Scotty' Lavell had a right reputation down there. But this weirdo who was in strange clothes like a hippy gone wrong had the cheek to talk back to me.

'Fuck off,' I said.

'Come on, gimme my money.'

'Bollocks.'

It went on like that for a bit, and this kid kept starin' at me. He was a big bloke but he was dressed weird as shit. Anyway, I just snarled at him and moved off.

It was only years later that I realised I had been turning into the same kind of bully as Steve and his mates had been at school. They picked on me 'cos I was different and I was pickin' on this kid 'cos he was dressing different and chose to be different.

So I'd like to apologise to him, and he knows who it is, 'cos it was George O'Dowd who later became Boy George. I reckon I owe him a week on the door for free whenever he's playing. The offer's open, George – sorry about that one, mate.

It was around that time I decided to take up boxing 'cos you could do it down St Peter's Youth Club. So it starts off, first week skipping, second week shadda' boxing, third week sit-ups and push-ups which I was doin' all day long anyway. Well, I'd had enough of all this and said to the trainer, 'Pat, I wanna do some fucking boxing!'

He looks round the place and says, 'Do it with Les.'

I thought, Great, I can hit someone now. This is what I've wanted to do for ages.

So I get in the ring. Pat says to take it easy and move around. I'm doing it – jab, jab. This black kid two years younger than me goes – *bang*! – straight on me nose. So I'm moving around – bang, bang, jab. Then – *bang*! – another one on me nose. I'm thinking, He's done that twice, I don't like that. So I'm coverin' up – jab, jab – and then he hit me again. Fuck this, every time I try and go for him he hits me on me fucking nose.

That was it – bollocks to it – I was gonna stick to judo in future. Anyway, the bloke I was fighting, Les Stewart, who was only about 14 then, later emigrated to Trinidad and became light-heavyweight champion of the world. He had forced me to give up boxing. If Pat had given me a different opponent at the beginning *I* might have become light-heavyweight champion of the world. But that was the end of me boxing 'cos I thought I wasn't any good at it. Thanks a lot, Les.

Judo was my real big love and I was managing quite a high standard. Girls I didn't have time for, and then one day I met Sheena, who would eventually become my wife. It was at a disco at a hall in Eltham. She was 15 and I was 18 and my mate says, 'Have you seen that girl over there? She's the best looking one here.' So I've had a look and he bets me he can chat her up before I can. We had a bet and, for about six months, I followed her to different places, kept asking her out and she kept saying, 'No, no, no.'

Then on Valentine's Day I managed to get a date with her at the pictures. I was standing outside and I'd waited 20 minutes until I'd had enough and I was about to go. But as I was leaving, she turned up. I says, 'Why are you late?'

She says, 'I wasn't late, I was early. I was waiting round the corner to see how long you'd hang around for me. Twenty minutes ain't bad. Shall we go in and see the film?'

We hit it off right from the beginning but there was one thing I didn't like telling her about. I was ashamed to let her know I couldn't fucking well read or write. I thought if she found out, she'd drop me like that.

But I couldn't hide it from her and one day she twigged when she found me looking at the Charles Atlas course I'd bought. I was trying to figure it all out just by looking at the pictures. It was the same with me other bloody body-building books. Great pictures, but I didn't know what the fuck I had to do to get a body like that.

In frustration, I turned to Sheena and blurted out, 'I'll never develop meself, Sheena, 'cos I don't know how to do the exercises. I can't bloody well read the books.'

She was an absolute darling. 'Don't worry,' she says. 'I'll teach you.' And she did.

I'd look at the pictures in the magazines and she'd read out the words until I eventually started recognising 'em. Most kids might have started with bloody farm animals, but the first words I started to understand were 'abdominals', 'biceps', 'hamstrings' and 'calves'.

And when it came to writin', she'd make me write down my body-building work-outs and diet over and over again. 'Reps' must have been one of the first words I ever learned to write. Me mum and dad were well taken with Sheena.

By this time, me training was really coming along. With Sheena's help, I was getting fitter, putting weight on and I'd joined a proper gym. I was pissed off with the Charles Atlas stuff. I was 6ft and 71kg. I was still very slim but I was wiry and my judo was getting so much better I started entering small tournaments. I had about five fights, won 'em all and I got into the final of this tournament. Who should I be up against but Neil Adams, who later won the silver medal at the Olympic Games.

He had already got a reputation and I thought, I don't stand a fucking chance.

He had come from Manchester to train down in London and I just kept thinking, Shit.

So we're on the mat and I'm pushing him and pulling him and I think, This is easy, I'm gonna beat him today. But, in fact, he was leading me into a false sense of security. The bugger reeled me in. He dropped his guard, let me come in and – *slam*! – we were on the ground. That, of course, was his speciality, but I didn't know it at the time. He spun round and he got me into a strangle. And I thought, I ain't gonna give in with all these people watchin', I'm gonna get out of this …

And then I thought, What are all these people doing in my bedroom? And then I could hear the faint sound of something that was familiar but I couldn't place it … I'm looking round … How many fingers can you see? … the sound getting louder … a rhythmic drone … I was going under again … I was going down again … Neil Adams had taken me out. He had strangled me until I was out cold, until I could hear that bloody sewing machine. And once again it was a nice experience. It was a weird feeling, the rush, the euphoria … And that was the only time I've ever been knocked out.

But even though I'd lost to Neil, I was beginning to impress a few people, and one of 'em was John Madden who, at the time, was top doorman in London and was, and still is, one of the nicest blokes you'll ever meet.

He sent a friend of his named Don Austen, who was better known as Don the Docker, 'cos he worked at Tilbury, round to see me at the gym where I was building meself up and pressing some good weights.

'You Stilks?' he asks.

'Yeah, who wants to know?'

'You doin' anything tonight?'

'Not a lot.'

'Wanna come over to the Music Machine and earn yourself some money?'

'What've I gotta do?'

'You gotta make sure Sid Vicious comes to no harm. He's doin' a personal appearance.'

I thought, Wow, Sid Vicious … Sid Vicious from the Sex Pistols. I've gotta make sure no harm comes to him.

Yeah, and then I realised … wasn't he the one that was thin as a pin, white as distemper, had a major smack habit, and used to like ripping his chest open on stage.

Yes, *that* Sid Vicious.

I thought, Fucking hell. Make sure he comes to no harm! I'm probably too fucking late.

2

THE FIRST DOOR OPENS

**NO MAN HAS FEAR ...
UNTIL FEAR COMES TO HIM**
STILKS

THE FIRST ONE HIT ME JACKET. DON HAD ASKED IF I HAD A WHITE SHIRT AND BLACK TROUSERS. WELL, I HAD, BUT THEY WERE GOING A BIT GREEN NOW. SPLAT! ANOTHER ONE HITS. THEY WAS SPITTIN', POGO-IN', ATTEMPTING TO STAGE BOMB, AND I HAD ONLY ONE SET OF ORDERS – IF THEY TRY TO RUSH THE STAGE, STAMP ON THEIR FINGERS AS HARD AS YOU CAN. I WAS READY ... I WAS READY TO PROTECT SID VICIOUS!

The Music Machine, or the Camden Palace as it's been named a few times, is a huge 1930s building opposite Mornington Crescent at the bottom of Camden High Street in North London. It had originally been a theatre and was opened by Ellen Terry. It was fucking massive and lit up. I was impressed.

Inside, it was like a bloody rabbit warren. I was introduced to John Madden who was then head doorman and he showed me round. It was just corridors everywhere you went. We ended up at the VIP bar, got introduced to the guy who ran the place, Mick Parker, and then I was shown where to stand on the stage. I had the best spot in the house, but when Sid came on it looked like the whole bleedin' place was about to go off. They went bloody mad. Jumping in the air, spittin', Sid lurchin' around the stage, music deafenin'. It was complete bedlam and then the first of the fans tried to get on the stage. I spotted him, straight over, ground his fingers into the floor and he dropped back. Everybody was gobbing and it looked like I was in the front line of attack. But if I thought I was having it bad, I only had to look at Sid. What a bloody sight! He looked as if he was about to keel over at any minute.

I can't remember how long the appearance was, but it wasn't very long, and then Sid lurched off. The crowd was milling around, stampin', shoutin', pissed out of their heads, and we had to herd 'em out into the street. I pitied the poor pedestrians. Of course, I managed to get lost in all them bloody corridors and the next thing I know I'm somewhere near backstage where this bloke who I'd met earlier told me to guard this door and not let anyone in.

'It's Sid's dressing room,' he whispered. 'Don't let a soul in, passes or no bloody passes.'

So I'm religiously guarding this door. 'Sorry, mate, can't go in there, private ... I don't care what you say ... No fucking entrance ... now go back from where you came.'

Most of 'em didn't bother to argue, except for this small half-stooped sort of guy. 'I'm Sid's mate.'

'Yeah, and I'm Johnny Rotten's fucking half-brother. Now 'op it,' I says.

'No, this is genuine, I've got summat for him.'

'I won't tell ya again. 'Op it.'

'Just tell him Eric's 'ere.'

'Mr Vicious doesn't wanna be disturbed.'

It went on like this for a while and I thought will I have to drop him. John Madden hadn't told me what to do in cases like this. But eventually the geezer scarpered, threatening to be back in a few minutes with someone who'd vouch for him.

'Take as long as you like, mate,' I said, ''cos you ain't going to get in here anyway.'

Then suddenly the door opened behind me and there was Sid, completely wiped out of his head, rolling his head, starin', tryin' to speak but not making it. And then he suddenly shouts, 'Anybody seen my fucking dealer? Where's the fucking dealer? Eric … Eric … ! Fucking bastard's let me down again. I'm getting outta here.'

To this day, I'd like to think that by refusing the bloke entrance backstage, I'd saved Sid from coming to any harm. But I hadn't – he was dead in a couple of years.

At the end of the night, John came over and asked me if I'd enjoyed the show and would I like to do it again the next night because Toyah would be playing? I said, of course I would. Remember, I was still only bleeding 18 years old.

And then John handed me £15. I was amazed. I thought just being there was payment enough. But no, I was on to a little earner.

The crowd for Toyah were nowhere near as fucking out of it as they had been for Sid, so I don't think I trod on any fingers that night. But it still turned out to be fucking weird. There were all these fans in strange black clothes and spiky hair.

Toyah's sister introduces herself to me and asks if I'm enjoying it and would I like to go 'back' to meet Toyah after the show? I says, 'Yeah,' and when it's all over we head backstage. Blow me if it ain't the same dressing room that Sid was using. I thought, Here we fucking go again.

The dressing room looked like your usual pigsty with plastic cups, half-eaten sandwiches and general litter everywhere. But there was no sign of Toyah and I suppose I must have looked a little disappointed 'cos her sister says, 'What's the matter?'

'I thought we was goin' to meet your sister. Where is she?'

'She's over there,' says Sis, pointing.

'Where?'

'There, look.' And bugger me, she was pointing at this open coffin in the corner. And inside was Toyah! My stomach went funny. I thought, Oh my God, what on earth's going on.

Her sister says, 'Don't worry, she ain't dead. She just likes resting in coffins, she feels very relaxed. She sleeps in them sometimes.'

And I thought Sid was weird! It was a fucking 'mithtery'!

This was turning out to be a right apprenticeship. But after the first few shows, John said I was ready to work on the door. There were about half-a-dozen of us, including an ex-heavyweight British boxer, but John still wouldn't let me get into any bother because of me age. Even if I went to the toilet, one of the other blokes would come with me to make sure I wasn't picked on. Maybe if I had had it 'hard' early on, I wouldn't have ended up doing 25 years on the doors. I might have got me head kicked in or got stabbed. These guys were old-time bouncers; they were showing me the way to get into the job. Nowadays, you can do a course and get a certificate saying you're a doorman, but that's no substitute for going through an old-fashioned apprenticeship. I didn't go into the bigger scraps with blood and stabbings for quite some time. But there had been a couple of murders at the place before. Lenny McLean, the Guv'nor, had been working there at the time. In fact, I was asked to work there because Lenny had moved on. I was his replacement, although he was at the top of his career and I was just learning.

We used to move all the people out of the Music Machine in layers. First the dance floor crowd, then the first floor, and so on. But one night there's this fucking bloke in the bar who refuses to move. I'd asked him three times and then didn't know what to do next. So I ask this other doorman, and he just says, 'Do what you think's right.'

I says, 'Do I hit him?'

'If you feel that's what you have to do, then hit him.'

But I was still worried about whether I was a bully. I had never hit anyone for no reason. But I thought, OK. I'd told him three times, and he was still moaning on about not moving 'til he had finished his drink. So I just went *bang*! into the stomach, just the one with me right, and he hit the wall and slid down.

I looked at the other doorman. 'Did I do right?' I asked.

'If you think so.'

That was the first time I ever hit someone professionally.

* * *

While I was starting to learn me trade, Mum and Dad were moving up the property ladder.

The house in Wickham Lane was up for grabs at £11,000 and we moved into a £19,000 home in Cumberland Avenue in Welling. It was a better area, a better house. It was still a terraced house with three bedrooms, but it was a lot more modern – it had a bathroom.

I was still going down to St Peter's Youth Club. I didn't drink or smoke because I was more into looking after me body. I had dreams of being a champion, even a fucking wrestling champion. I could see meself as Mr Universe. I was pumping weights, curling, pressing, all the time getting bigger and fitter.

We didn't have much money when we were down the Youth Club and we needed 'pennies'. So there were three or four of us who would do these fucking petrol stations.

Sometimes it was the same three, sometimes others. And 'cos none of us drove, we'd walk out the youth club to the end of the road and jump on the first bus that came, it didn't matter which direction. We didn't care what bloody number it was or where it was going. It was the first bus that turned up. We'd sit on the bus for 20 or 30 minutes and then we'd get off and go through this ritual. First everyone had to empty their bleedin' pockets.

'C'mon, let's have all your money,' I'd say. 'The lot.' The guys would hand over all their cash. It wasn't a lot. And I'd add mine and then I'd throw the bloody lot over the fence. Then none of us had any money. So we couldn't get home by cab or by bus. That meant we had to do the job. We had to look for the nearest petrol station.

In those days, they weren't alarmed and there were no cameras. We never used guns and we never used iron bars or anything like that. It was our physical size we used or the fact there were a few of us. Garages were usually manned by only one person.

So we'd walk in and pretend our car was broken down and then ask if they had a petrol can we could borrow. While he was looking for the can, we'd be looking round to see who's here and what's happenin'. It gave us time to suss the place out quickly. If there was no one there, we'd 'ping' the cash register and that'd be open. If he was comin' back, one of the others would stop him and push him into the back room and stay there with him. We'd put all the money in a bag and that'd be it. But on one of the jobs, a car pulled up …

'Don't panic, leave this to me,' I said to the other guys. 'You keep him quiet in the back room,' I pointed to me mate, 'and you two lay down under the counter.'

The geezer enters and comes to the counter.

'That'll be £5 please,' I say, fairly shitting meself. But he paid up and we all breathed a big sigh of relief. Fuckin' hell.

'Come on, let's get out of here,' I shouted at the others. And I told the bloke in the back room, 'You move out of there in less than five fucking minutes, and I'll be waiting outside to hit you on the head. And you won't like it.'

Then we'd leg it to the nearest bus stop, jump on whatever bus came next, and then we'd get off at a train station. We'd take the first train to London and then we'd wait to get a train back home. The best number we ever pulled was £2,000 and, remember, that was more than 20 years ago. It was a fucking lot of money.

One of the lads who used to go down the youth club, Rob Wireless – I'll never forget that name – knew that petrol stations were our thing. He said he'd got this job at a petrol garage, and we thought, Lovely.

He said, 'I'll be working there on Thursday and what I want you to do is, you come up, rob me and I'll make sure there's money in the till.'

With the big garages, Esso or Shell or whatever they were, they used to have these chutes which would send the money underground to protect it, and there would only ever be a few hundred at the most in the till. He was gonna keep as much money as possible back for us to take and then we'd make sure there was a good drink in it for him afterwards.

So at about six o'clock in the evening on that Thursday we got the little team together at St Peter's Youth Club. We got to the garage and walked up to Rob. 'Hi boss, give us the money.'

He said, 'I haven't got enough in here yet.'

So I walked round a bit, had a look at a few sunglasses, picked them up, then out the door and down the road. Ten or fifteen minutes later, we went back and asked him for the fucking money. Again he said, 'There ain't enough here yet.'

I thought, That's strange. But we walked out again, waited, went back in and then I shouted, 'You gonna give us the money, Rob, or not?'

He looked a bit nervous and then said, 'Yeah, but not today, not today.'

So we walked out. I thought, All right, fuck you.

Then I hear 'Aaaarghhh!', and I see this guy running towards us screaming and wielding a pick-axe handle. I thought, Fucking hell! and we started running the opposite way. But there were three other bloody blokes running towards us! I'm thinking, They've found out we were doing the circuit, the garages, and that fucker Rob has put a local firm on us. This is what's goin' through me head. He's grassed us up to the company that own the petrol stations and because we've taken a bit from quite a few of 'em, they've put a firm on to us. So I said to the boys to turn round and go for the bloke with the pick-axe handle first and take him out. So we're running in the other direction now, and this black cab pulls up. And over the top comes a gun.

'STOP! STOP!'

The guys that are chasing us arrive. They smash right into the legs first, then the chest and we're knocked to the floor. I'm rolling around a bit trying to find something, any fucking thing, to hit back at 'em. But they've got us pinned down, and then they grabbed us and threw us all into separate cars. I went into the black cab with the guy with the gun and I'm thinking, Fuckin' hell, where the fuck are they taking us?

'Hey, what the fuck's goin' on?' I say.

'Shut up.'

'Where you takin' us?'

'Shut up.'

I thought, Right, they are goin' to do us over. What are the odds here? I've got one on each side and there's the driver. The odds weren't very good at all. So you can imagine, the biggest relief of my life was when we drove into Eltham Police Station. They weren't a firm after all – they were the Old Bill.

They hadn't said a bleedin' word to us yet and we were thrown into separate cells.

I was in there two days. There was no food and I didn't know if it was day or night. No one had spoken to me, not a word. Forget all that bollocks about being able to phone a solicitor or your mum or your fucking auntie. There ain't no bacon, egg, sausage and beans and a cup of bloody tea like you see on *The Bill*. There's nothing.

Anyway, this CID bloke's come down and he tells me all me mates have confessed that I'm the ringleader. Now you got to remember, we ain't got no money 'cos we didn't rob the garage, and all our other cash had gone over the fucking fence as usual. We didn't have any guns or iron bars but they had hit us with pick-axe handles and pulled a shooter on us. So I don't know who was the most scared, us or them! I knew one of the other guys in the gang really well, we grew up together, and I knew he wouldn't grass me up and call me the ringleader.

So I say to this CID bloke, 'Look, I haven't done anything. I went in there to buy a box of chocolates for me mum.'

'So it took three of you to buy a box of chockies, did it?' he says. And with that he threw me back in the cell. No more questions. Again, nothing to eat, nothing to drink, left us there for another day. Eventually, we were all dragged out of our separate cells and charged with 'conspiracy to rob', I think it was. The charge sheet detailed what we had on us, like a set of keys and that, and then at the end … one iron bar.

I say, 'I ain't signing that.'

'Why not?'

'I didn't have a fucking iron bar.'

'Yes you did. We found it in the gutter. You must have dropped it there.'

'Well, I ain't signing it.'

So he crossed out the iron bar and I signed the charge sheet as close as I could to the writing so he couldn't put the bloody iron bar back in later. We all pleaded guilty to conspiracy because we didn't get a solicitor and didn't know any better. We were hauled up to the magistrates' court in Woolwich the next day and I think we got a small fine. You see, while we had been at it for some time, we had never been caught, and this time we hadn't done nothin'. We were there to rob but didn't manage it. Rob kept putting us off because he didn't think the Old Bill had arrived yet. What did he fuckin' think was gonna happen – bloody police turn up with a great big fucking sign saying 'HELLO, WE'RE HERE'? That's why he was dodging it, and kept tellin' us to come back. But the police were there all the time.

The next day, we went looking for Rob.

'What's the idea of fucking setting us up then?'

'I never set you up.'

'Yes you fucking did and then all this happened.'

'Well, if you think that then let's have a straight'ner, let's have a fight.'

I said, 'I'll fucking give you a fight. Let's go over to the block of flats round the back.'

I told Scotty to stay there with Rob's mates.

Rob throws a couple of lefts. I've got hold of him, and throw him on to the floor with one of me judo throws. Got him in an arm-lock, put it on, and begin to apply pressure.

'Did you grass us up?'

'No.'

'DID YOU GRASS US UP?' I'm shouting, all the time adding more pressure on to the arm-lock.

He's screaming now. 'Yes I did. Stop it, Stilks, stop it. It wasn't my fault I had to …'

Bash! While I've got him in the arm-lock, I smash my fist into his face. I was thinking I'm gonna give him bruises all over his face to let other people know he is a no-good fucking grass. So I'm hitting him with me right and he's screaming.

I'm shouting, 'Who's the fucking king round here?'

'You are, Stilks, you are.'

So I just left him there lying on the floor in agony.

A few weeks later, I was watching TV and they was doin' a programme on the Flyin' Squad. And it was the same team that done us for the petrol station. I thought, Bloody hell, they were taking us seriously. That must have been a big operation. Felt a bit proud about that.

But it put me off crime for ever. Not because of any moral reasons. It was just like everything else, except judo – I was no fucking good at it.

* * *

I was still seeing Sheena at the time and me readin' and writin' was improving. But I don't know how she put up with me 'cos I was more interested in me mates and me judo and training than I was in girls. I was a bit spotty at the time and didn't have a lot of confidence. I don't think I ever went out with her on her own. It never crossed me mind to do that. I'd invite her to come to the pictures but all me mates would be with me as well. That's just the way it was. I was still only 19.

I used to love playing cards with the boys as well. I could play cards for days and I remember one Christmas, must have been 1977, I was meant to meet Sheena at my house, the one in Wickham Lane, 'cos she was bringing the presents. I thought it would be all right, me parents would let her in and she could sit there and wait for me. So I carried on playing cards and at three o'clock in the morning me dad turned up with Sheena.

'Wassup, Dad?'

'You're what's up, my boy. Sheena here has been sitting on the doorstep with Christmas presents waiting for you since six o'clock last night.'

I had this theory that the less I saw of her, the less we could argue, so the relationship would always go well. Me friends had relationships with girls and they were always breaking up and I thought it was because they was seein' 'em too often. I would only see Sheena twice a week and, if I took her out, me mates would come, too. I don't think we spent a day and a night together for the first couple of years we knew each other. And I wasn't that interested in sex. I was more interested in fucking about. I only went out with one other girl at the time and that didn't last long 'cos she messed me about once and that was the end of it. You don't get a lot of second chances with me.

My dad thought I was turning into a right bleedin' tearaway and so I was desperate to impress him and show him I could do something. That was when I decided to enter this pool contest at the Royal Oak pub in Woolwich with the winner getting £100 – a lot of money. So I thought, Right, take Dad down there and show him how good I am at pool. There was me and a couple of friends entered.

It was an Irish pub, full of Irish, and things started off OK. Win a round, go into the next, win a round. I was getting up to the final bloody stage and I went to take a shot when my mate Baines said, 'Don't take that. Do it from the other side then you can come back on the other ball.' I thought, He's fucking right.

First thing I hear was from me opponent, 'That's cheatin'. You can't do that. He's told you what to do.'

'That ain't cheatin', I was gonna do that anyway. I was just takin' me time and thinkin'.'

'Nah nah, the game's void.' And he went to clear the table.

He was a grown man, so I turned me snooker cue round and hit him across the head with it. Anyway, it all kicked off and I can remember me dad sitting there looking forlorn and shakin' his 'ead slowly from side to side and sighing. I was fighting like mad, the place was in uproar, and Dad was quietly sitting there in the middle of it all.

Eventually it all stopped and me hand was fucking hurting. This geezer's got blood pouring down from his head, and the guv'nor, Tom, an Irishman, announces as calmly as you like, 'We'll play that one again.'

We did and I won.

Now I was into the final and I was up against me mate Baines. He was a brilliant snooker player and a much better pool player than me. Anyway, we were on the black ball and I remember he left me this hard shot with the cue ball up against the cushion. I couldn't pot the black directly and, for £100, most people would have played safe. But I thought, Fuck it, so I doubled the white ball off the opposite cush, it hits the black and down it went. The money was mine. A nice little earner, and we still talk about that game today.

* * *

If I was the tearaway, then my sisters seemed to be the opposite. As Greek daughters in an orthodox home they were restricted in what they could do. Dad was really strict. No boyfriends, no goin' out, nothin'. They were bein' brought up to be good Greek housewives. Even I took 'em for granted. I remember coming home with Sheena once to introduce her to me sisters. I was obviously showin' off a little bit and my youngest sister Maria happened to be doing the ironing that day. Being as cheeky as I was, I threw her me underpants and said, 'Iron them.'

'I ain't ironing them.'

'Yes you are. Dad says you've got to learn to iron everything.'

So she calls me over and goes *bang*! with the iron on me arm and for the next fucking few months I was walking around with bloody sergeant's stripes. I realised then that my sisters had a rebellious streak in them and all Dad's strictness was only stokin' it up.

Sheena and me sister Maria got on really well together. I think it's 'cos Maria, who was very bloody fiery, knew how to take me down a peg or two and Sheena liked that. They got on so well they even both worked at the same hairdressers in Woolwich once. That's when Sheena saw how fucking fierce Maria could be. They used to wash these old ladies' hair, but if our Maria didn't get a big enough tip, she'd go into one. Once she said to some old dear who never tipped, 'Would you like a cup of coffee, madam?' And then she proceeded to pour the coffee over the fucking woman's head and massage it into the scalp like it was shampoo. That's how strange Maria was getting.

It was about that time that my Gran, my mother's mum, came to live with us. She always wore black – head-to-toe black. A typical Greek Cypriot woman, she would sit in the corner in her own world. She knew fuck all about Britain and didn't want to know.

I remember once I was off to Cyprus and Gran says, 'Stellakis, can you bring me back a radio from Cyprus?'

'What the fuck for, Gran? We've got radios. Listen to one of them.'

'No, you don't understand, Stellakis.'

'What don't I understand?'

'I need one like we had in Nicosia. So I can listen to the Greek programmes. You can't get them on these radios you've got over here.'

And she never changed. She rarely went out and never understood where she was. We used to take her to church and then when we got back, we parked Dad's little car across the road. Then we left her there for a joke. She was completely bewildered, didn't have a bleedin' clue where she was. Just turning around looking this way and that, completely lost. She was right opposite the house but she had never been on the other side of the road before.

We were always playing jokes on Gran, but we loved her, really, and would not let any harm come to her at all.

I was still working at the Music Machine in Camden but it meant having to cross London to get to work. One day, this bloke came up to me at St Peter's Youth Club and said, 'Hey, can you get me 16 doormen?' The Students' Union were promoting gigs at the Woolwich Poly and the head doorman had died of a heroin overdose.

I remember Slade played there and some other big names but by now I wasn't interested in bloody popstars, I was interested in earning money and in any way I could. Popstars meant fuck all to me. As far as I was concerned, I was the most important person there.

I was on the door and thinking how I could get some money. Bainesey was there to help me. As the people came in, I would rip their tickets in half and give 'em half back. Now listen, you could learn somethin' here. After you've got a few half tickets in your hand, you no longer need to rip up a ticket. As it's handed to you, just fold it in half, palm it into the bottom of your hand and give 'em back half a ticket you've ripped earlier from the top. I knew those bloody nights I stayed up playing cards would come in handy!

The organisers were everywhere, so me and Bainesey had to play this one very carefully. There I was ripping and palming tickets until I got quite a few whole tickets in me hand. I wasn't interested in who was number one on *Top of the Pops*. I only wanted to know how much I was gonna earn that night. While no one was looking, I'd give Baines all the whole tickets and he'd go off down the road.

'Have you got tickets for tonight's show? It's all sold out. Just a few more left here,' he'd shout at the punters. 'Come on, get 'em quick, only a few left.' He was brilliant at being a tout, and we quickly started making money.

One night, one of the other bouncers at the Woolwich Poly comes up to me and says, 'Stilks, there's a bloke trying to get in with a dog.'

I say, 'Well, you can't fucking well let him in then, can ya?'

'I know, Stilks, but he's blind.'

So I went down there and explained to him, 'There's not a lot of room in there, mate, and you've come to see the band.' Then I think, Oh shit. 'Sorry, mate, I meant you've come to *hear* the band.'

He says, 'Look, I just want to pay me money and come in. If you want to look after me dog.'

'Oh, for Christ's sake, just come in and do whatever you fuckin' want,' I said.

Later that night, I was counting me money on the door and realisin' that at only 19 years old I was a head doorman. But with head doorman comes responsibility and you have to take charge of every situation. You've got to lead from the front. If you don't, someone else will take your fucking position. You have to make sure you're running the place and be seen running it. When it kicks off, you have to be the first one in and take the ringleaders out first. I told the other bouncers, 'If it goes off in the street, don't bother. We've got to make sure it's all calm and quiet in here. Is that understood?'

Obviously it wasn't, 'cos it kicks off in the street when some idiot bloke hits a girl, and one of me guys goes running out of the Poly into the fucking street where they're going bloody mad. Then it kicked off. Someone's down and some other fucker's stamping on him. Then our bloke's down and they're all kicking him. So I've said, 'We've got to go out there ... we can't leave him out there.' My mate's said, 'No fucking way.' So I've gone out there, pushed 'em off and grabbed him. 'You all right?' I stayed with him; anyone coming to hit him, I've gone *bang*! and they've gone down. I've looked over there, and another one's gone down. I'm thinking, Fucking hell, I'm doing well today. Then they all start runnin' away and I'm thinkin', Wow, I'm really getting into this. That's when I turn round and see Nick Nettley, who later became Lenny Mclean's minder, standing right behind me. He would be about four or five inches taller than me and he was like heavy duty. His huge hands were up in the air and he was moving them around. It was like some giant growling gorilla was standing behind me and I hadn't noticed. He trained to be London's strongest man. He turns over cars, pulls lorries, bends iron bars. And here he was behind me, growling at this fucking mob. No wonder they was running in the other direction. And all the time I thought it was me. I thought they was terrified of me, but nah, it was Nick that put the fear of God into 'em.

Blokes was falling over to get away, others were hurt and lying in the street. Some were holding their heads. And then out of the Poly comes this blind guy being led by his dog. The dog was skilfully weaving the blind bloke round the injured on the floor.

'Enjoy the show did ya?' I asked him.

'Very much,' he said. 'So happy there was no trouble.'

No fucking trouble! It was like the battle of the bloody Somme. But I'm glad he couldn't see it.

* * *

In those teenage days, trouble seemed to follow me wherever I went and I swear I never started it. But Dad didn't believe me and Mum was exasperated. Only Sheena seemed to keep an open mind when I told her how I'd hurt me hand again or why there was a bruise here or there. Looking back, Sheena was a real treasure and I still don't know why she put up with me because she didn't really deserve the way I was treating her.

But trouble was following me around and I literally couldn't get on the bus to escape it.

When we was bored with St Peter's Youth Club, we used to go to another one called Harvey's in Charlton where they had a sort of disco on a Thursday. When it finished, we all got on the bus back. At the time, there used to be this estate in Charlton full of yobbos and one night they decided to get on our bus to cause some aggro. I was upstairs with the lads; they came upstairs and the conductor asked them for their fares.

One of 'em said, 'Bollocks, we ain't paying ya nothing, mate.'

So the conductor pulls the cord and says, 'Right, this bus isn't moving until you pay.'

The bus is sitting there and I turn to one of the yobbos and say, 'Look, lads, pay your fare and then we can move on.'

'Who the fucking hell do you think you are?'

With that, another one shouts, 'Smash the bus up.' And they've started kicking the windows in. Out goes one of the windows, followed by another. There's glass everywhere, all the girls are screaming as they get off the bus. All the passengers downstairs thought they were surrounded by fucking nut cases and started climbing out the windows which had been kicked through. Then there was only me and this other fella standing there and he's gone, 'C'mon then!' So I think, Fucking hell, what am I gonna do?

So I ran towards him, grabbed him and dragged him down. With that, his mates came back and began taking the light bulbs out of the bus and smashing them over me head. There's blood pouring out of me head and I'm thinking, I'm gonna be fucking cut to pieces. They were only tiny nicks but they don't half bleed a lot.

The police arrived and blocked off the road and started arresting all the yobbos. Of course, they went to arrest me but the bus conductor stepped in and explained that I was the one who told 'em to pay their fare. I just slipped off quietly and managed to get back home only to hear me dad go, 'Stellakis, have you been fighting again?' It wasn't worth explaining that I was only trying to help. By now, I had been in so many skirmishes at the Music Machine and at the Woolwich Poly, who was gonna believe me when I said I never fucking started nothin'?

* * *

I've never been sentimental. There was no time for that. The way we'd been brought up, you had to be hard to survive. All right, I'd been in a bit of bother with them petrol stations and stuff but I never carried a weapon and never hit anyone. Anyone that got hurt, got hurt 'cos they fucking well deserved it. But for the first time in me life, I was starting to think that I was being dealt a bad hand every time the cards got shuffled. Dad was ashamed of me, even though as the only son and eldest child I wanted to be a credit to him. Mum, well, she didn't say much. She was too busy looking after us all and making sure there was enough food on the table. I was still her little Stellakis, the boy with the bad ear. The boy who nearly drowned and almost frightened her to death. Like all mums, she'd stick by her kids no matter what happened. But what the fuck was gonna become of me?

I was sitting outside in our little garden in the Cumberland Avenue house in Welling thinking about all these things, just staring into space, when Sheena comes up to me.

'Penny for 'em?' she says.

'Nah, I'm not thinking of anything.'

'Don't lie to me, Stellakis, there's something worryin' you, isn't there?'

'Nah.'

'Go on tell me. A trouble shared is a trouble halved.'

'There ain't no trouble, I'm telling ya. I was just thinking about me future that's all and, you know, what's gonna happen to me. I won't be a bloody teenager very much longer and Dad's expecting me to buck me socks up and do something. And I don't want to let him down.'

'And what big ideas have you got then?'

'Well, that's it, see. I haven't got many ideas. Either big 'uns or small 'uns. And that's 'cos I ain't got no money.'

'But what if you did have money, Stellakis, what would you do then?'

'That's easy, I'd open me own gym. I'd become an Olympic coach training all the other guys at weight-lifting. And I'd compete meself and get honours and bring 'em back for me mum and dad to see that I could make somethin' of meself. That's what I'd do. But it's no use dreaming, I gotta get down the Poly and get on earning some money.'

That's when Sheena reached out to me and whispered, 'It's good to dream. When you're from the working class, sometimes that's the only thing you have to keep you going.'

And she kissed me lightly. And for the first time, I felt a surge inside me and I held her tight and we kissed long, passionately and properly for the first time in my life. Whatever my future was going to be, I knew that Sheena would play a part in it, a big fucking part in it.

3

ALL CHANGE AT THE STATION

BEND THE RULES AND IF THAT DOESN'T WORK, BREAK 'EM

STILKS

'**S**TILKS! ... STILKS! .... OH, GLAD I CAUGHT YA. I'VE GOT A BIT OF BAD NEWS,' SAID THE GUY WHO HAD BEEN ORGANISING THE GIGS AT WOOLWICH POLY. 'YOU'RE NOT GONNA LIKE THIS, MATE, BUT WE'RE GONNA STOP PUTTING ON BANDS DOWN HERE. IT JUST AIN'T WORKING FINANCIALLY, KNOW WORRA MEAN? SOMEHOW, WE NEVER SEEM TO BE MAKING ENOUGH MONEY TO COVER ALL THE OVERHEADS. THERE'S PLENTY OF PUNTERS COMING IN BUT THE PROFITS AREN'T GOOD ENOUGH. I'M SORRY ABOUT THIS, STILKS. YOU'VE BEEN A DIAMOND GEEZER LOOKING AFTER THAT TEAM OF YOURS AND HANDLING THE DOOR, BUT I'M AFRAID THAT'S IT, MATE. I HOPE IT HASN'T COME AS TOO MUCH OF A BLOW.'

Too much of a fucking blow? I was amazed it had kept

going for four months, considering the money me and Bainesey had been making with our little ticket scam.

So I had to find another earner and, as we had moved to Cumberland Avenue in Welling, I thought I'd have a walk down the High Street and see what kind of pubs and clubs there were around. I walked down the road, done a right, and the first pub I came to was the Station Hotel, big fucking boozer on the corner. There were a couple of guys at the front door and me, being full of meself, I just go, 'If you get any trouble in here, lads, give me a call, I'm having a drink in the corner, and I'll help ya out.' I stayed for about three-quarters-of-an-hour, and on me way out one of the guys who turned out to be the landlord asked me if I'd done door work before. I said, 'How much a night and how many fucking nights?' I think it was about £15 a night, seven nights a week, so I took it 'cos it was only round the corner.

It was a no-jeans, no-trainers type place and only for people over 21. If only they'd known the security wasn't even old enough to get in the bloody place! And for the first three years, I was there all on me own and had to deal with all the situations meself. One of the first ones that cropped up taught me a bloody good lesson.

It was a rainy night and I was standing on the door when this gentleman tries to come in and I've had to stop him.

'Terribly sorry, can't come in, no jeans.'

'But they're expensive jeans.'

'Look, mate, I don't care if they're made of fucking gold

thread, it's no jeans. I'm not interested, I don't own the place, I only work here.'

So he says, 'Do you mind if I stand here and wait for me friend to come?'

'OK, you can wait there, outta the rain.'

But what I didn't realise was that he was there lining me up. I was still young at the job and didn't twig it. As he appeared to move off, he turned round and *bang*!, he hit me straight in the eye. It shook me and, by the time I'd composed meself, he was out the door and running up the road and too far for me to give chase. But that's a lesson I've never forgotten. If I turn anyone away from the door for whatever fucking reason, they have to go. I don't give two shits whether it's raining or bleedin' snowing out there, they have to go. Once you've told people they can't come in, then there is no reason for them to be standing around. It's a lesson that's held me in good stead.

There was another pub over the road opposite the Station called The Plough where all the fucking rough lot used to drink, the building types that wore jeans and boots and couldn't get into the Station. So one night they came over, and they were in their thirties while I was still about 19, and I say, 'Sorry, lads, you ain't coming in.'

'What you gonna fucking do about it?'

'We'll see, but you ain't coming in. You do what you think you have to do and I'm gonna try and stop ya.'

I push one of 'em up against the wall and another one back through the doors. Remember, these were grown men.

I didn't think anything about the incident until a few nights later when they tried to get in again. But this time they'd got the right clothes on and I couldn't keep 'em out.

'Enjoy your evening, gentlemen,' I said, and went back to keeping a watch on the door.

Only minutes later, it kicks off inside. I'm on me own and have to be really careful about how to approach the situation. It's gone off in the corner and I'm over there quickly in time to see one of these guys from The Plough sticking a screwdriver into the bloke he's having an argument with.

First he jabs it into his arm, then it goes into his leg. I try to keep 'em apart.

'Get fucking back,' I say. 'What the fuck is happenin' here?' Then this guy holds the screwdriver up to me face and it's not looking good.

'Look, Tony, it's your mate from the other night. The one that threw you out,' he starts taunting. 'Whaddya think we should do with him?' And then he puts the screwdriver blade on my cheek and starts slowly pushing it.

'Want some of that do ya, mate?

I say, 'Yeah, think you're fucking hard do ya? You and all your fucking mates and me on me own. Go on then fucking do me, go on. There's six of you and only me on me own, so go on and do what you fucking wanna do.'

With that, the guy with the screwdriver glanced for a split-second at his mates but that was long enough for me. I've got his wrist and turned the screwdriver away from me face.

Then I twist as hard as I can, applying as much pressure as possible and he slowly loses his grip on the screwdriver which falls to the floor. Another of his mates goes to pick it up and I thought, I'm not 'avin' any of this, and, quick as a flash, I resort to me old Sid Vicious trick and me steel-capped boot comes down with as much force as possible on his hand. I've probably broken it from the sound of the yelling. But it did the fucking trick and they all ran out of there with the usual, 'We'll be back to fucking kill you.' Strange that, 'cos I never saw 'em again.

The bloke they had been stabbing was more shocked than anything. I took him to the back of the bar and we cleaned him up a bit and bandaged his arm and leg.

At home, I never mentioned the sort of things that went on in me line of work. Gran, sitting in the corner as usual all in black, never realised I was a doorman and used to think I dressed up in a black jacket and bow-tie 'cos I was always getting invited to posh dos.

In fact, I had to have quite a few dinner jackets, smart white shirts and bow-ties for obvious reasons – sometimes I'd come home from working on the door and there'd be bloodstains on the jacket or shirt. I'd be forever having them cleaned and putting on a fresh set of clothes. Wearing a dinner jacket and that isn't just for show either. OK, it says to the people wanting to come into the club or pub that it's a posh place and they'd better watch their manners. But it is also psychologically intimidating. It says, look, we are not only dressed the best but we are all dressed the same, we're a team. Try taking on one of us and you take on all of us.

Of course, Gran didn't know anything about that and no one was going to upset her by putting her straight. She'd give me her sincerest blessings from all the Saints for being smart and handsome and then she'd say, 'Oh, Stellakis, all dressed up like that. Off out on a date are you?'

'Yes, Gran.'

It was best she didn't know what I got up to.

The Station could hold 500–600 people all drinking, shoulder-to-shoulder, so it's no wonder things were going off all the time. But I got a fucking routine working where I could literally clear the place in three minutes using the same technique John Madden had taught me up the Music Machine of moving them around from the back and hustling them out like cattle. Three minutes was my record for getting 600 people out of there. Not fucking bad. I think they must have made up the 20-minute drinking-up rule years later just to get at me.

One night it was heavin' in there and I'm on me own and I hear – *smash! smash! smash!* – all these glasses breaking, so I've run in and saw all these young blokes smashing each other up with glasses. So I've got hold of one by his hair and started dragging him and throwing him out. Then, as quickly as possible, I'm back inside and I drag another one of the fuckers out. But I'm thinking, Christ, with the crowd and the fight goin' on, I'll never be able to tame the place on me own.

That's when this geezer at the bar, a local face named Kevin Wishart, sees that I'm gonna be in a bit of a fucking pickle. So he comes over to help me and grabs one.

'Evenin',' I said as he hauled some yob out of the door. So there was the two of us yanking 'em out of the crowd and throwin' em out the door.

Nothing more happened at the time. But about three years later, when I'm emptying the bar again, this bloke walks in eating a kebab. He comes up to me and he goes, 'Do you remember me?' And I'm really good with faces. Names and places I can forget, but faces, never. So it dawns on me it's this fucking bloke I'd thrown out by the hair years earlier. He had got much bigger.

So I went *bang*! and landed a left on him and he went over.

'Yeah, I fucking well remember you,' I said.

Well, what was I supposed to do? I could see he hadn't come to offer me a bit of his bloody kebab. He was with two other burly guys as well and they were looking for trouble.

As he got up, I say, 'And you can't consume food here that hasn't been bought on the premises. So fuck off.'

* * *

It was about this time me sisters, Yianoula and Maria, decided they had had enough of Dad keepin' 'em under his thumb all the time. They were teenagers and they were going to rebel in the only way they thought would work – they ran away from home.

They didn't leave a note, nothin'. One day, they just didn't come home from school.

'Can't think where your sisters are, Stellakis,' said Mum glancing at the clock. 'They should have been home half-hour ago. Hope nothing's happened to 'em.

'Don't worry, Ma, they're probably doin' summat at school. Be home soon.'

'Hope so. It's not like them, they're usually such good girls.'

Another hour went by and Mum started getting more and more worried. 'I've told them time and again to come straight home from school,' she mumbled. 'Your dad'll be here soon and what's he going to think?'

The key went in the door and, as Dad appeared from work, Mum rushed at him and shouted, 'Andreas, it's the girls, they haven't come home from school.'

'Have you phoned the school?'

'You know I don't like that phone.'

'Give it here, woman.'

And with that, Dad phoned the school only to find they had left at the normal time. With that news, Mum suddenly started moaning, complaining about chest pains, while Dad phoned the police.

Lot of bloody use they were. Probably nothing, they said. Probably with friends, they said. Turn up in a few hours, you'll see, they said. What they really should have said is: 'We couldn't fucking care less.'

So Dad decided he would go in search of them himself. He had got himself a little car by then and was driving up and down the streets looking for his daughters. He was looking in burger bars, local youth clubs, all the places he had forbidden his daughters ever to enter.

But it was no good. They were nowhere to be seen. Nobody slept that night and Dad had the next day off work to continue his search. The tension in the house was at bloody boiling point. Mum's chest pains got worse and she started crying; Gran kept asking what all the fuss was about and I was pissing meself laughing.

It went on for three days and then the phone rang. It was Aunty ... Yianoula and Maria had contacted her to try and make the peace with Mum and Dad. They had been staying around the Peckham area with a friend. They had made up a pack of lies about being thrown out of the house and everything.

Anyway, they came back home and it was anything but sheepishly. They had made their fucking point. They wanted to be treated like other English girls, and Dad was clever enough to realise if he didn't give them more freedom, then they would run away again – and this time it would be for good.

I was still stopping the ragged ones from coming in the Station Hotel and throwing the bloody rowdy ones out. There was the usual ruckus on a Friday but I was handling meself well, the judo was going fine and everything had settled down at home again. Gran slept in the little box room, Mum and Dad had their room and me sisters had theirs. I used to come home late from the Station Hotel so I'd sleep on the floor downstairs. But I didn't care – I was seeing Sheena more frequently and I'd discovered the joys of sex. So had Yianoula.

When she actually said it, I thought a fucking nuclear bomb was gonna go off.

'Mum, Dad,' she said as calmly as possible, 'I'm pregnant.'

There was a long silence while everybody looked at each other and then everyone started talking at once, blaming each other. My mother wanted to know how she would look the neighbours in the eye; Dad was ranting about the shame she had brought on the family name, it was complete bedlam. Of course, she would have to have an abortion.

'No, I won't,' insisted Yianoula.

'You bloody well will,' said Dad.

'What's goin' on?' shouts Gran, who couldn't grasp the situation.

'It's Yianoula, Gran, she's pregnant,' says Maria with a certain glee, 'cos she knows whatever she does now, she can't be as bad as her sister.

It went on for a few days until everyone started to calm down a bit. Dad decided that whoever the boy was that had got Yianoula pregnant, he would have to do the bloody decent thing and marry her and she would have to bring him home to meet the family.

'What's his name?' asked Mum.

'Mark'

'That's a nice name. Where did you meet him?'

'Does it matter, Mum, does it really matter?'

'Well, you'll have to bring him home to meet us.'

'OK, anything you say, but I'm keeping this baby.'

Anyway, the day arrived when we were all going to meet Mark. And Mum, bless her, went to extra lengths to get the house nice and clean, and brought out the best china. Everything was set.

So the door bell goes and Yianoula rushes to open it and then ushers Mark into our tiny front room.

Gran looks as if she's about to faint; Dad freezes with his mouth half open and Mum starts to blurt out, 'He's … he's …' and then suddenly stops herself.

So I finished what she was going to say in me head, '… fucking black!'

I don't know what Gran was so upset about, she wore fucking black all her life anyway. But from that day forth, she would never look Mark in the face. Whenever he was in the house, she would shield her eyes with a newspaper.

Someone had to break the ice, so I shook his hand. 'How ya doin', mate?' I said. 'Don't mind this lot, they got some barmy ideas.'

Mark turned out to be one of the nicest, hard-working blokes you'll ever know.

I remember, though, when they got married and Mark's dad got up to make a speech, he mentioned that when they met Yianoula how shocked they were to find she was fucking white.

* * *

Back on the door at the Station Hotel, the same night that I'd met Mark for the first time, I was in a real dilemma. Over the road was this bloke with his kid about four years old, and three lads had come up to him and started shouting at him. I'm looking over thinking, OK, could be a problem. But, of course, I'm not here to sort out the fucking world's problems. I'm getting paid to keep a clean bloody orderly house at the Station. Anyway, these lads start pushing the bloke around and his kid bursts out crying, but I think, Nah, they ain't gonna hurt him, and anyway it's nothin' to do with me.

But suddenly they knock off the bloke's glasses and stamp on 'em. I thought it was going too far but there were three of them and only one of me. And, anyway, they hadn't actually hurt him. But then they pushed him to the floor and started kicking him while the little kid was crying for his mummy and I thought that at any minute the kid would get caught up in the bother. The kid went hysterical and I thought, I'm not havin' that, it's gone too far. He's now crying, 'Daddy, daddy', and these fuckin' louts are laying into the guy.

On the back of the door at the Station there was a huge metal chain that they used to hold the door open. So I pulled it off and went outside swinging it. I'd flex my biceps and swing it harder. It's cutting through the air in faster and faster circles. I'm warming it up, and it's whistling around nicely.

I've crossed over the road. 'Come on, then, you cunts, you wanna pick on someone, try fucking me.'

And with that I've caught one with the chain, and it's going that fast it wraps round his back and chest. I pull it – he's gone straight down. *Bang*! I hit the other one, and he's gone over. The third one ran away. I pick the bloke up to find out if he's all right and ask him, 'What's all this about then?'

'Thanks, mate. I was just sitting in a burger bar with me son and they started putting ice down the back of my little boy's neck and, because I told them off, they were waiting for me outside.'

'Right, well, you'd better get goin', mate,' I say. I was worried now in case anyone had seen the incident because I could have got nicked for it. As it happened, it was OK and the last I saw was two of the louts picking their fucking mate up off the floor and he kept collapsing as they took him away. I reckon he had never been hit with a chain before.

I was easing meself into the job at the Station and time was going by pretty quickly. The family had recovered from the shock of Yianoula being pregnant and had got to like Mark. Just when everything seemed calm, I decided to tell 'em my piece of news.

'Mum, Dad, guess what? Sheena's pregnant.'

This time, the reaction was more of a resigned shrug, as if it was only a matter of time. They had always had me down as a bit of a tearaway, so nothin' really surprised 'em any more. After Yianoula, Sheena's pregnancy was a softer blow to 'em.

In fact, it was Sheena's mum and dad that hit the roof this time. As far as they were concerned, there was still a big stigma to being unmarried and pregnant. Mr and Mrs Wheeler were divorced by then but they both went mad, called her all the names under the bloody sun and threatened to disown her. At one point, Sheena and me were seriously facing the prospect of being out on the streets. But we thought, Bollocks to the lot of 'em. It was going to be our baby and nothing could stop that. If anything, it was binding us closer together and I even used to go with Sheena to the baby clinic. There were all these pregnant women and me, a great big hulking bloke by now, sitting there in the middle of 'em all in the waiting room.

One day, the nurse called us in. 'Miss Wheeler, Mr Stilks, I've got something to tell you. There is a very slight chance because of the light bleeding that Sheena may not go to the full term.'

'Whaddya mean?'

'Well, there is just a possibility that she may miscarry and that's the reason why we want you to come into hospital, Sheena, so that we can keep an extra eye on you. It's nothing to be alarmed about.'

So Sheena packed a few things and off she went to West Hill Hospital in Dartford where every fucking gynaecologist and obstetrician, or whatever they're called, seemed to want to see her. They'd examine her, mumble, huff and puff and stand in the corner nodding. The problem was that Sheena was very big for her date of pregnancy and everyone was wondering whether she was going to give birth to bloody twins.

'It's difficult to tell,' said one doctor who I thought was being paid a bloody fortune to tell exactly that. But I kept me mouth closed. 'It could be twins, although I don't know … maybe … anyway, Miss Wheeler, we have decided to give you a scan just to sort things out.'

It was when Sheena was having the scan that the nurse turned the monitor away from her and just said, 'Your pregnancy has ended.' There was no fucking explanation, except that a specialist would come and see her and she had to wait. She was four months pregnant and the size of someone seven months gone.

We were totally shot through, devastated. One minute we thought Sheena was having twins and the next nothing, and no explanation. I'd been over the moon at the prospect of bein' a dad. People had been suggesting names for the baby and everything, but I wasn't interested in all that, all I wanted to know was whether the baby was fine. But my bubble had been well and truly burst. And poor old Sheena was totally in shock. Instead of the doctors and nurses comforting her, they wheeled her out into the corridor and left her there. Bloody National Health Service.

I remember it was ten o'clock at night before they got hold of a specialist who could tell us what the fuck was going on. It was a Mr Wolfson and he said, 'I'm sorry, Sheena, but you have suffered a hydatiform mole pregnancy. It is an extremely rare condition. In fact, you stand a much better chance of winning the pools than you do of having this type of pregnancy,' he smiled. 'But, sadly, it means we will have to induce labour and you will have to give birth because the pregnancy was so advanced.' He kept talking and I was just pacing up and down.

'What was he on about, Sheena?'

'Oh, Stellakis, it's terrible,' she started crying silently. 'It seems the placenta has grown so much it has engulfed our little baby and sort of smothered it or something. Oh, Stellakis. Inside me is just a malignant growth now and I've got to give birth to it anyway.'

This mull pregnancy lark was so rare that they asked Sheena if she would mind all these students being there when they induced the birth. They said it might be the only chance they would have in their lifetime of seeing such an event. Well *they* could fucking well watch 'cos I wasn't going to.

First, Sheena was put on a drip for a couple of days to induce the labour and what was funny was that they were constantly bloody well assuring her that she would be all right. I kept thinking, Well, why shouldn't she be all right? Loads of births are induced all the time.

Anyway, she was wheeled into this theatre where all these students and doctors could get a good look at her and the growth – as I prefer to call it – was induced. It was the most hideous thing you've ever seen according to Sheena. It didn't resemble a human baby, it looked like a big bunch of bloody grapes.

It was one of the most heart-breaking episodes in my life. But I picked meself up and tried to carry on by working at the Station and keeping busy. I was still throwing 'em out and keepin' 'em bloody well out. In fact, I was getting so good at it now, I was about 23 by then, that I even managed to throw one bloke out of the door while I was holding a tea-cup and saucer. He got fucking booted out and I didn't even spill a drop of tea. That was the incident that made me a bit of a legend round Welling. Everyone wanted to know if it was true. And I swear to this day it was.

But if I was trying to keep my life going, it was harder for Sheena. The whole thing had devastated her. But she picked herself up as well and opened a hairdresser's shop called Odysee. It was a new beginning. We had grown closer together and we was goin' to put all the bloody past behind us.

Sheena still had to go to West Hill Hospital for check-ups which I suppose were routine, although looking back I remember thinking they were a bit odd. They used to give her a really thorough check-up, including X-raying her. I thought, What the fuck are they X-raying her for when all she has done is lost a baby? Ah well, I s'pose it's all for the best.

Sheena was proud as punch about the hairdressing salon. It had been open a week, maybe two, custom was building up, and she was doing fine. Then one day, just as she was doing one old dear's hair, she could feel herself slightly bleeding which turned into haemorrhaging quickly and badly. She rushed home and phoned the doctor only to have his bloody secretary say, 'I'm sorry, he can't see you today. Phone tomorrow if you're worried.' By now Sheena's starting to panic and she phones the hospital.

'Look, I've had this mull pregnancy,' she says, 'and now I'm starting to haemorrhage, am I all right?'

'Well, your doctor's secretary has gone home, but don't worry,' was the reply.

Poor old Sheena was curled up in a chair at home trying to calm herself down, thinking maybe she'd been over-reactin'. Anyway, I arrive at her house with me mate Andy Barber and see what a right state she's in.

'What's up, love?'

'Well, it's a bit embarrassing really,' she said, but then explained what had happened.

So I thought, Right, I'll show that bloody National Health Service. So I picked her up, put her in the back of Andy's car and took her to West Hill Hospital. I was playing merry hell with 'em. 'My girl's ill,' I shouted. 'She's had one of the rarest pregnancies you fuckers have ever seen and you don't give a shit about what's happenin' to her now.'

It seemed to do the trick 'cos I soon had doctors and nurses runnin' here and there, and the next thing I know they are getting Sheena ready to wheel her into the operating theatre. This was the bunch of wankers who, an hour earlier, had told her not to worry because the doctor's secretary had gone home. I was pacing up and down, bloody angry about the whole thing. If this had been the Station Hotel, I'd have been throwing the fucking lot of 'em out.

Sheena came out of the theatre where they'd managed to stop the haemorrhaging and said they'd examined her to make sure there were no complications after the mull pregnancy.

About a week later, things was settling down again when Sheena had a phonecall, from Charing Cross Hospital this time.

'Miss Wheeler?'

'Yeah.'

'It's Charing Cross Hospital. We've had the results of the examination and tests you took at West Hill and we'd like you to come and see us.'

'Why's that?'

'Well, we think you may need a little hormone treatment following your pregnancy. I wonder if you could actually come in and see us tomorrow.'

I thought, Well, at least something's fucking getting done at last.

The next day, me and Mrs Wheeler went with Sheena up to Charing Cross where she had to go through another examination. And this time it was every tiny part of her body from the top of her head right down to her toes that got examined. The works. So me and her mum are waiting for the examination to end and I notice there are lots of people walking around with no bloody hair and I could feel me heart sinking and sinking. The doctor had us in. He was quite a nice young chap but I could see he was going to have difficulty.

He quietly said, 'There's no easy way to tell you this, Sheena, but we think you would benefit from a course of chemotherapy.'

Cancer.

Fucking cancer.

* * *

Strangely enough, I wasn't really devastated by the news. It's such a bloody enormous thing to take in I just kept thinking, Well, she's in good hands, in a good hospital. I'd visit her every day, stay a couple of hours and then go back and work at the Station. It was like living in two different worlds. At Charing Cross, there were all these doctors and nurses working round the clock to save people's lives, dishing out medicines, calming people down. They were doin' everything they could for my Sheena.

Back at the Station, it was fuckin' bedlam. It seemed like every night somethin' was goin' off. And it was always some yobs causing it. Like one night when these three bloody skinheads decided they didn't wanna drink up after time had been called.

'Come on, gentlemen,' I say. 'The place has closed and it's time to leave.'

'We ain't finished,' says one of 'em. 'We're staying.'

'Now, I won't ask you again. Leave the premises.'

'Nah, what ya gonna do about it?' says this fucking cocky bastard.

So I say, 'Nothin'. Fine. Carry on. This is your third warning.'

After three warnings on private premises, bouncers are allowed to go in. I was in.

They knew somethin' was up and kept giving each other darting glances. I'd called their bluff and so I went and told one of the other blokes that was also working on the door that night to lock the front up after throwing out all the punters. Then we both went back into the bar.

'Hey, what the fuck's goin' on?' says one of the yobs.

'Nothin'. You wanted to stay. Now you can stay. We're staying, too,' I said, as I pulled myself up to my full height and started flexing.

Crash! The table went flying as all three of them tried to make a run for the door. I got one of them by the wrist and pulled him back.

'Sit down, scum. I thought you wanted to stay and finish your drink.'

First, they pretended to play it a bit hard. 'Yeah, and who do you think you are?' and all that ritual I've heard a thousand times before. Then one of 'em stooped and put his hand down to his shoe and I knew he was going for a blade. This was it. He screamed out in pain as I connected my boot on his ankle. Down he went, hitting his head on a chair and passing out. There was just time for me to grab one of 'em going past with one hand, while my mate had got hold of the other one.

'What shall we do with these then?' he said.

'Dunno. Maybe we should knock their heads together, knock a bit o' sense into 'em.'

'No, please,' shouted one of the skins who was now a trembling wreck. 'We're goin', we're goin' now.'

'But I thought you wanted to stay?'

'Please, please.' They were pleading now.

'OK,' I say to the other doorman. 'After three.' We got a grip on each of them and pushed their heads down like a battering ram. 'One ... two ... three ... *Crack*! And they both fell down to the floor along with their other mate. All of 'em out cold.

'Well, it looks like they are staying after all,' I say to my mate. 'But they ain't getting no fucking breakfast in the morning.'

* * *

To show my appreciation of the good work the doctors and nurses were doing for Sheena, I thought I would raise some money for the hospital. And what I did was get everyone to sponsor me to walk from my house in Welling to Charing Cross Hospital one Sunday afternoon. And all the money I raised I was planning to give to Professor Bagshaw who was dealing with Sheena at the time.

Now there's a couple of ways you can raise money. You can bully people into it and shame them in front of their friends, so they'll feel guilty if they don't contribute, or you can quietly tell them what you're doing and they offer to sponsor you out of respect. That's the direct method, that's my method, and it's easily the best.

In those days, I used to enjoy walking and I'd always have me fucking army boots and green fatigues. I remember once walking up Ben Nevis. We had a bit of a race and I remember scrambling through the clouds and beating Nick Nettley to the top. Another time, I decided to walk to Margate with me mate, Pierre, down the A2. We got 37 miles down the road before we got kicked off it.

So a 13-mile walk up to the hospital was bugger all to me. I was fit, and I was training to do a half-marathon at the time because I thought running was easy, running was for poofs. I did the fucking half-marathon in one hour and 42 minutes. It was a Grade 1 race, the Maidstone Half-Marathon, up and down hills. The walk to London was along the flat so it was just a stroll to me. But respect to all runners, 'cos you just don't know how hard it is.

A friend of mine, Mark, who's emigrated to America now, walked with me and I can remember him moaning all the way. He was a bit of a fat lad, about 15st, and all he wanted to do was stop and rest and have something to eat.

I kept saying, 'Come on, Mark. Sheena's waiting for us. We said we'd be there by three o'clock.'

I had to keep pushing him along. 'C'mon, Mark, get a fucking move on, mate.'

Anyway, I cajoled and shouted all the way until we finally arrive at Charing Cross Hospital in Fulham Palace Road.

'Can we use the lift now, Stilksy?'

'Don't be such a prat, Mark. The idea was to walk all the way from my house to Sheena's bed. No, c'mon, take the stairs.'

'But she's on the top fucking floor, Stilks.'

'You get your arse up them stairs.'

By the third floor, Mark was beginning to flag but I kept on going, counting the steps as I carried on.

'Eighty-nine … ninety … ninety one.'

And there I was outside Sheena's ward. I'd made it all the way from home to see the girl I loved.

I burst into the ward beaming, ready to show Sheena just how much I cared for her. I went straight up to her bed. 'Shee …' I looked around … the bed was empty.

'Ah, Mr Stellakis,' said one of the nurses. 'Sheena's just gone to the toilet. But don't worry, she is expecting you!'

I thought, 'Blow me down. I've walked all this way – and just missed her'.

Sheena was in hospital for three months straight and then she was allowed out at weekends for about three months while still having the chemotherapy and lumbar punctures and one thing and another. Then she became an outpatient and went in once a week. All told, it took about a year of specialist and top-class treatment before my Sheena was better. So I'm glad I was able to raise £2,500 for the hospital. Mind you, the Government should be fully funding the hospitals, then they wouldn't need fucking charity. Bloody National Health Service.

But I was the happiest bloke around when Sheena was able to come home at last, although Professor Bagshaw did warn us about one thing. 'Don't get pregnant again for at least three years, Sheena,' he said. 'You can't be too careful.'

Although Sheena had only had the hairdresser's for two

weeks before she was taken ill, the landlord let us get out of
the lease without any penalty when I explained the
circumstances. And with Sheena now on the mend, we
decided we had to be together. So we took a look at the
fucking property market, to see what we could afford. And,
of course, we couldn't afford fuck all. Not with the poxy
wages I was on down at the Station. Sheena got a
hairdressing job but that wasn't very well paid and both
wages amounted to bugger all when it came to buying
property. We were getting the right hump cos we couldn't
buy anywhere so I think, Let's jack it in and go and put our
names down on the council list.

But then I'm walking down Erith market and I see this
property that needs doing up. It needed a lot of work on it
and was just around from her mum's. It was up for £16,000.
So me and Sheena went and had a look at it. It still had gas
mantles on the wall that you light, no bathroom, an outside
toilet. Obviously, an old couple had been living in it and it
really was in a bloody poor state. It was a small terraced
house. It had three bedrooms but one of 'em you had to
walk through to the other. But I was determined it was
going to be ours – 11, The Nursery, Slade Green.

Although it was run-down we couldn't afford anything
else and so we decided to go for it. I managed to raise a
£1,000 deposit and then the bloody fun started. It needed an
extension built on the back for a bathroom; it needed a new
roof, rewiring and replumbing.

I took the ceilings down, I took the floorboards up; I took

the plaster off the walls. I knocked out the fireplaces and the wall between the living room and the front room. Because we didn't have any money, I had to get my friends to help me – in fact, I think I still owe 'em a drink. We even changed the windows. The whole job took about a year and we had to live with our parents while the work was going on.

That's why whenever we move house now, Sheena says, 'Hope I haven't gotta move back in with me mum.'

I'd promised Sheena the world when she came out of hospital. But it looked like, once again, I wasn't going to be up to providing it, even though I was working all day trying to get the bloody house ship-shape and all night defending the Station against all-comers.

There was a ruckus all the time – I'd started to forget how many fucking times I'd smashed up me hand on one little toe-rag or another. And you just try repairing a run-down old house when your bloody hands are smashed, bruised and broken!

Smack! That's the extension won't get done for another few weeks. *Bash*! I'll never be able to lift them window frames now. *Christ*! His head must have been made of cast iron. Now how was I gonna skim that new plaster on the walls? It was like bloody Fort Apache some nights down the Station.

So one day I thought, Bollocks. It's about time I put me and Sheena first.

So I proposed to her.

I can't remember what I said. But the answer was 'Yes'.

4

THE
SCHOOL OF
HARD
KNOCKS

**JUST BECAUSE YOU CAN'T SEE AIR IT DOESN'T
MEAN YOU STOP BREATHING.
JUST BECAUSE YOU CAN'T SEE GOD IT
DOESN'T MEAN YOU STOP BELIEVING.**
STILKS

DRRRRRRR ... DRRRRRRRRR ... DRRRRRRR ... MUM HAD GOT HERSELF AN ELECTRIC SEWING MACHINE.

'I thought maybe I could help making the wedding dresses,' she said, being the well-meaning mum she was. As I shuddered inside, she added, 'Not Sheena's, perhaps, but some of the others. It would help cut the cost.'

And she was right. It was going to be costly. It was awful. I married the same woman twice!

Being Greek Orthodox, if you marry in an Orthodox church then it ain't legal by British law. And if you marry in a British register office, it ain't legal by Greek law. So we had to do it twice. First came the register office, and then we had a little 'do' back at 'er mum's, which was fine. But then about six months later, I married Sheena again at a Greek Orthodox church in Welling ... and it nearly didn't go ahead 'cos tragedy struck.

Just before the white wedding, I heard a bump in the house and rushed to see what had caused it.

'Mum,' I said, 'quick, Gran's fallen down the stairs.' And there she was, lying in bloody agony at the bottom of the stairs. All dressed in black she was.

We called an ambulance and she was carted off to hospital, and they told us she'd broken her hip. Sadly, the old dear didn't pull through and she died just a week before we were planning to get married.

'That's it,' said Dad. 'You can't go through with the wedding in circumstances like this.'

'But, Dad, everything's been planned. Everything's arranged. We gotta carry on with it now. It was gran's last wish we should get married.'

Anyway, we argued the toss and Sheena and me had the last say, so we went ahead with it. I just wish I'd listened to Dad. It turned out to be a nightmare. I gotta say, it was the worst day of my life, and I wouldn't ever get married again.

There was loads and loads of organisin' and we had to pay for most of it ourselves 'cos Sheena's mum was divorced and didn't have lots of money. My parents obviously didn't have fucking bucketfuls either. They all helped with the food and that, and Sheena and I paid for her wedding dress – she wanted one out of a shop!

The wedding day was the only time I've ever fucking got anywhere on time. So I'm there outside, waitin' and waitin'. Ten minutes, twenty minutes, half-hour, three-quarters-of-an-hour. Everybody's turned up. Where's the wife? Oh, fucking hell, I thought, she hasn't changed her mind? I was waiting anxiously, half the people were asking what had happened; most of 'em wanted to go home.

An hour after she's supposed to be there, she turns up.

'Wassa matter, Sheena?'

'We lost the ring.'

'You wha'?'

'Well, Dad turned up in this chauffeured car to bring me here and we slammed the front door and got in the car. It was only after we were nearly here I realised we didn't have the ring and had left it in the house.'

'Oh fucking no way,' I go.

When they got back to the house, they found they had left the keys inside as well. So the chauffeur, a bloke named John Maggott, decided he'd have to break into the house to get the ring. You can imagine the fucking scene. Everyone dressed up to the nines; Sheena in her wedding gown and the geezers with bleeding carnations in their buttonholes – and one of 'em trying to get in through a window they'd found that was slightly open.

I held my head in me hands and counted up to ten slowly.

'Whaddya do then, Sheena?'

'Well, he managed to get in and open the door and I found the ring. Then we raced back here.'

Strangely enough, the ceremony itself went without a hitch. All the best men – known as Gumbarros, who sign the ribbon as witnesses in a Greek Orthodox ceremony – had to pay some money for the privilege, as did the best women. I thought that was a bloody good idea! But things weren't gonna last. We all piled back to this hall for something to eat. We had invited about 200 people and about 300 bleedin' people turned up. There ain't enough tables, there ain't enough chairs, there ain't enough of anythin'. So I've gone to some of the guests, 'Have our fuckin' table.' So now I'm all stressed out, me and Sheena have got nowhere to sit, we're eating standing up, all that's gone on.

And then it's Greek tradition that the groom has to start to dance. Well, I don't dance! I say, 'Hard bastards don't dance.' You'll never catch me dancing. But, anyway, if you want to have money pinned on you in the Greek way at weddings, you have to dance for it. But I don't wanna fuckin' dance. I'm getting more and more stressed; I don't have a table. I'd paid all this money, all this food, all this drink and every other bastard's enjoyin' themselves apart from me. It was *my* day – I'd paid for the fucking lot. Imagine £3,000–4,000 in them days. Now they wanted me to dance for me fuckin' money, I'd got nowhere to sit and I was goin' mental.

'C'mon, Stellakis, dance … dance …'

'Son, it's tradition in Cyprus – you must dance.'

'Hey, Stilksy, shake a leg, mate.'

And then it started, the fucking funeral march for all non-dancers – Zorba the Greek.

I can still hear the music goin' through me head. The rest of it's a blur, arms in the air, knees bending. I probably fucking fell over but I don't know. It's all on video and I've refused to watch it from that day to this.

And you have to be careful where they're pinning that fucking money on ya.

Married bliss. Bollocks! Me mum had got rid of me bed because we were supposed to be moving into the house we'd bought. But, of course, it wasn't fucking ready. We couldn't move in, so Sheena stayed with her mum and I moved to my parents'. Every night after work, I would go back and fall asleep on the floor. It went on for six months. What a bleedin' way to start married life.

* * *

Throughout the Eighties, the level of violence increased dramatically around South London. I went from being the only guy on the door at the Station to having to recruit new blokes all the time until there was a real pack of us working there trying to keep the scum out. And that's when my career as Britain's most respected bouncer started to take off. Of course, I didn't know at the time that I was creating a fucking legend for myself but that's exactly what I was doing. As head doorman at the Station, and the man with most experience, managers from other bars and clubs would seek me out and beg me, 'Stilksy,' they'd say, 'we can't borrow a couple of your guys can we?' Or, 'Stilks, mate, you couldn't find us anyone permanent could you ... only we've been having a bit of bovver lately?' And my reply was always the same, 'How much?'

As you know, ever since the bloody days down at Woolwich Poly, I've always been fond of me little perks. And this one was a fucking treat.

On Fridays and Saturdays, there was a little charge of £2 to get in the Station which I thought was a good idea. You got a ticket from the kiosk. Tom who ran the place would let in about 500 people and then shut the kiosk up and go inside.

Then we'd have a fucking go.

'That'll be two quid, sir … Don't worry Tom, he's just been out.' Another two quid. 'He's been out and come back, Tom … two quid.'

And then we'd share the money amongst the doormen. Tom and his wife Tia knew what was going on but they used to turn a blind eye. Of course, things got out of hand when Tom came out to the door one time and noticed that we had a bigger queue going than the official one at the kiosk.

'It's not what you think, Tom. This lot have been out once and now I'm searching them again,' I'd say.

Of course, as the fucking place got more crowded and popular I had to hire more doormen and suddenly the money we were nickin' wasn't enough to go round so I came up with another idea.

Tom and Tia went out on Tuesday night and, as soon as we'd waved 'em goodnight, I'd get Max or one of the guys to open the kiosk. We had a little key cut and we were away. It was supposed to be fucking free entry on Tuesdays, but not any more. As far as we were concerned, it was £1 after 8.00pm. It was a really bloody successful idea and Tuesdays became known as our 'bonus night'.

On a Saturday night, it used to get really busy but there was no way we could do a lot o' nickin' until Tia decided to put her mum in charge of the kiosk. She was a proper dithering old lady. There were all these people queuing up.

'Get your money ready,' I'd shout. 'Got the right money? OK.' And then I'd get one of the doormen to kick the kiosk as hard as he could. 'Don't worry, Ma,' I'd shout to Tia's mum, 'Just a bit of trouble going on out here, nothin' to worry about here.'

But she'd be petrified, pull down the shutters and close the kiosk with herself inside. Then we'd go to the punters, 'Two quid, please, have the right money, two quid please, walk straight in.'

We were pulling so many stunts like that the brewery became suspicious and wanted to know why the bleedin' Station wasn't making more money. That's when they decided to put in another manager to try and sort things out.

He was a big fella named Mark Leeds, about 18–19st and stood about 6ft 4in. Big fucker. He's come in and I'm head doorman and, for whatever reason, he doesn't like me and wants to get me out the fucking way. But he doesn't know how to do it because I've sussed him and started behaving meself.

One day, about a month after he's taken over, he comes to the door and says, 'Stilks, I don't think we need you any more.'

'Whatcha mean, don't fuckin' need me any more?'

He goes, 'We don't need a head doorman, everyone's gonna be equal from now on.'

'OK, you don't fucking need me then, you fat cunt,' I shout, and then I push him up against the wall in the corner and go *bang*! *bang*! *bang*! into the chest and belly about half-a-dozen times.

'All right, Stilks,' he screams. 'Don't hit me no more, don't hit me … You can keep your job.'

But it was all videoed and he warned me that, if I did it again, he was gonna hand the fucking tape over to the Old Bill.

Anyway, I didn't think much more about it – he'd been sorted – until about a month later this guy named Brad turns up. He had this frightening voice like a giant and he was big as well, thick-set, 18st. I worked with him for a couple of weeks and he didn't seem a bad fella. But one of the other doormen comes up to me and says Mark's got this bloke in to get me out, the idea being to get rid of me and make Brad the head doorman.

So I thought, Fuckin' hell. I couldn't be seen to get beaten or walk out with me tail between my legs in front of my lads 'cos I wouldn't get another bloody job if that happened. If Brad somehow fucked me off, then no one would employ me.

In situations like that, there's only one thing you can do to save face. I walked in late that night on purpose so all the other doormen were there.

'All right, Brad? I need to have a word with you … in the toilet, it's personal.'

So we troop into the toilet and I go, 'Brad, I've er …'

Smash! I hit him before I even finished the sentence. He's dropped on to his knees but I hadn't knocked him out. He was a huge cunt. He staggers back up against the urinals. I'd used surprise on him but he was so hard I hadn't downed him and now I've got real fucking trouble on me hands. I saw that look in his eyes, a look of someone whose dignity has been shaken but who is ready to come roaring back. I thought, Fuckin' hell, he's gonna kill me. He's wet from lurching back into the piss corner but that ain't stoppin' him. So I kick him as hard as I can – no fucking effect. I'm standing there, flexed, wondering who's gonna make the next move.

It's Brad. He goes into his pocket and slips on a huge knuckle-duster. I thought, Shit. But I could see in his eyes that he was still a bit dazed. The duster covered the whole of his right fist and, as he came at me, I dodged, moved around him and tried to get him into a stranglehold round the neck. The Stilks Strangle was a speciality. But he slipped out, went into one the cubicles and yanked the lavatory chain off. With the fucking duster and the chain he was tooled up, and he came at me again. He was starting to spin the chain, and he was snarling, that fucking giant voice was echoing round the tiled toilets, screaming that he's going to kill me. His arm goes up ready to bring the chain down, and that's my only chance … I'm in again, I'm up there. I'm fighting for my life, as I've always fought. This time, the Strangle is *on*!

With his neck in the crook of my right arm I start to put on the pressure, pushing his bastard neck to the left, using my left hand. It's going lower … lower … will it break?

With the Strangle on, any normal person should be unconscious in three seconds. I've got it on. I've got the Strangle on and me legs wrapped round him. No fucking hiding place now. It's on 100 per cent. The Strangle is so tight I've got no more strength. Then the cunt roars and bounces me against the tiles and tries to come up with the duster. But I'm still holding him.

So I says, 'I'm gonna kill ya, 'cos I haven't got the full Strangle on yet.'

But I'm thinking to meself, I've got it on all the way, I've got no more to give. His neck was so thick I couldn't get the force right in there and I'm thinking, Please God, let him go out, let him fucking well go down. Go out, for fuck sake's go out. But he wouldn't and he was bouncing me round the toilet.

So I shout, 'See that duster? I'm gonna punch you out and then I'm gonna fucking well kill you with it.'

Then some of his strength started to go. I thought, Thank God for that. The chain hit the deck, and I spun him. It was like a screwdriver, turnin' and turnin' as he went down. The duster came off and skidded across the floor. I grabbed the fucking thing. And then I said, 'Is this what you want?' *Bang*!

With that I walked out of the toilet, went up to the doorman who had warned me about Brad, smiled, showed him the duster and slipped it into my pocket. Then Brad came staggering out of the toilet with as much dignity as he could bloody well muster. He walked silently with his head down through the pub, past the doormen without saying a word and then he went. He never came back. That's how it is. Justice is very tribal. The winner stays, the vanquished fucking well leaves.

It was about this time, when I was getting well known and my reputation was building, that I opened my own gym. Things were going well at home. Sheena had fully recovered from the cancer that followed her pregnancy and, as the doctor had warned us, we left it for a few years before attempting to start a family. Fortunately, everything was perfectly all right and our daughter Emma was born on 19 April.

I was going to a friend's gym in Northumberland Heath and I bumped into this fella called Peter Hayford, who I hadn't seen for many years. We got talkin' and I say, 'I wouldn't mind openin' up a gym of me own.' He'd been thinking the same thing. So I said I'd go and look for a hall and, if Peter liked it, we'd go half each, 'cos, quite honestly, I wasn't that confident about doin' the thing on me own anyway.

I found the hall down in Crayford Way and Peter thought it was lovely but we were stuck for a name. But then we came up with this idea to call it PecS Gym. It stood for pectorals but the capital letters also stood for Peter and Stilks. We didn't have a lot of money and were on a really small budget. But as we got a few customers in, we used the money to run and buy a few more weights. This was strictly a weight-lifting gym, none of all that fancy nonsense they have these days. It was a basic place but it catered for all the people living in that area – and they were mainly skinheads. Politically, Crayford was very National Front. Nicky Crane, who used to run the British Movement, trained at our gym. He was on the front of the *Sun* for setting some poor fucker alight in Woolwich, I think. He got done for conspiracy, and I can't remember what the other things were, but he ended up getting four-and-a-half years inside. But I wouldn't allow any shit to go down at the gym. I made sure they all fucking well behaved themselves – skinheads, racists, whoever the fuck they were.

The only trouble I really had was when I was bloody stupid enough to take on this kid, Jim, who was there as part of the Youth Training Scheme. The gym was picking up and doing well and I thought, Yeah, let's get some kid in, and give him a break. He had been a bit wild and needed to be sorted out and he was interested in weights. He was doing well and doin' his training so I would run off to have me lunch and leave him there in charge of the money, phonecalls, and generally running the gym.

But I noticed that I suddenly started taking less money than I used to take and I thought, There's definitely summat wrong here. So one day, I thought, I know what I'll do. I'll get a bit of Sellotape, rip a £10 note a bit, Sellotape it together and put it back in the drawer. So I did that to all the notes.

That day I came back from lunch.

The kid says, 'Is it all right if I go now, Stilks?'

'Yes go on. Fuck off.'

Then he makes a big mistake. He says, 'You ain't got a fiver you can give me, have ya? I'm skint.'

'Yeah,' I says. And gives him the money out of me pocket.

Fifteen minutes later, I've opened the till, checked the money, counted the people in the gym and found there was a tenner missing. I thought, Right, I'm gonna find that fucker.

I got in the car and I knew the kid was a bit of a drinker so I went to his local pub. I walked in, looked round, couldn't see him, so I asked the barman, 'Is there a little fella called Jim here?' Then I saw him coming out the toilet so I goes, 'Jim, come here, mate, and fucking well empty your pockets! I'm a tenner short.'

'I ain't gotcha money, honest Stilks.'

So I goes through his pockets and find he's got some change and the fiver I'd lent him earlier.

'Where'd ya get that change from?' I ask. 'You told me you was broke.'

'Someone owed me some money.'

'Fucking funny, ain't it, 'cos someone owes me some, too.'

So I asked the barman to show me the money Jim had used to buy his round of drinks. He pulls this tenner out of the till.

I turned to Jim, 'That's my fucking money, 'cos I put the fucking Sellotape on it – see, you worthless cunt.' And I shoved the money in his face. 'What else you got hiding?'

And with that I lifted him up, he was only a small little runt, turned him upside down and started shaking him to see if there was any more money on him.

He was crying, 'Put me down, Stilks, put me down.'

'Not 'til I find out how much you've fucking nicked from me over the weeks.'

'Put me down, Stilks. Honest, I'll get the bleedin' money back for you. Honest.'

I thought, Shall I kick his head in while he's upside down? Nah, it wasn't worth it.

So I just let him drop. His head hit the bar room floor.

I turned to the barman and handed him back the Sellotaped £10 note.

'That's yours, I believe,' I said, and calmly walked out of the pub.

* * *

As the gym became more famous, people started coming from further afield; we had the British Skateboard Champion at the time. Then a couple of young kids came in – Peter Lane and Andy Kellard. They were like the tough guys of their school and they were training to get into the British swimming team so I started teaching them weights. They got stronger and stronger and Andy went on to become British Champion and win medals at the Commonwealth Games in Olympic lifting. If they didn't do as I told 'em, I wouldn't fuckin' well let 'em go home. If I set them a weight to be lifted, it had to be done. I'd lock the gym and wouldn't let them out. I'd hold them there and make them complete the reps. They'd hate it but they'd thank me afterwards.

Mick Wilson used to train there. I had done all the courses on the correct diet and taught people how to train correctly, so Mick and I used to train together. He worked there for me for a little while and later on he became Cobra in the Gladiators TV show and I ended up his best man.

As I was training other people, though, my judo went a bit by the board, although I hadn't lost my love for the sport over all the years. I was training at the time with Nick Nettley, who won the title of London's Strongest Man, and Nick used to wind me up 'cos he knew I would bite and he loves to get people goin'.

One day he said, 'How far did you get with your judo?'

'Brown belt. But I could have done me black any time I wanted.'

'No you fucking couldn't.'

'Yes I could.'

We ended up having an argument and I told him I'd prove it by going down the gym, polish up the judo a bit and that within two months I'd have me black belt. I didn't use my own gym but one in Dartford that's a school of excellence for judo. It was where the British team trained. It didn't take me long to get back into the judo – it's a bit like riding a bike – so I decided to go for my grading.

There are two ways you can get your black belt. You can do it slowly by going to different competitions and beating somebody by three points which is a Yuko; if you beat someone by a Waza-ari, that's seven; or an Ippon counts ten. If you win two fights – a seven-point and a three-point – you can go into another competition and that way you have to keep your points going until you get 100 points over two years and you'll get your black belt ... or you can go and do it the hard way. This involves taking a line-up of six different brown belts who are chosen for you by the British Amateur Judo Association. Fifty brown belts might turn up and they pick the six you had to take on in succession, and you have to beat each of them by Ippon which is a clean throw, a Strangle or an arm lock. You don't get no rest; it's just one fucking opponent after another.

Two of 'em I managed to get into a hold down and four of 'em went with the Strangle, or 'neck lock submission' as it's known in polite circles. The black belt was mine.

The Silks Strangle became one of the most feared weapons on the doors down in South London, as Brad knew to his cost. But, in fact, it was a pure accident that I started using that move at all in me job. It was all because over the years I started breaking me hands with too much punchin'. Me knuckles had been goin' and me fingers had all been broken so many times I thought, Right, that's it, I'm not fucking hittin' 'em any more, because at the end of the day it was me that was getting hurt. And that's when I started using the fearsome Stilks Strangle. Within three seconds, you're out cold. Most guys would struggle for a couple of seconds then they'd go under and I'd gently lay them on the floor. I remember one bloke I put out cold and when he started coming round one of the other doormen took him to the door to show him the way out. He started crying and saying, 'He's put me out … you've put me out.' He was so disoriented he didn't know whether he was conscious or not.

* * *

Usually after a particularly hard night on the door, some of the lads would come back to my place for a cup of tea. We'd moved from The Nursery and were now living in Oldfield Road, a more modern house and nicer area.

'Hello, darling,' I'd say to Sheena. 'Put the kettle on, Nick and a couple of the boys are here.'

So we were drinkin' tea when Sheena pipes up, 'Stellakis, I'm getting contractions every eight minutes.'

'Don't worry about it, love, just make another cup of tea.'

So me and the boys carry on talking. Nick Nettley can talk for bloody England, I tell ya, especially if it's about politics. There we are, setting the world to rights, when Sheena says, 'The contractions have come down to every five minutes.'

So I say, 'How do ya know?'

''Cos I can bloody well feel 'em. Now do something about it.'

'Come on, you're only panicking because it's your first baby. You don't know what you're talking about.'

So we have another cup of tea.

Then Nick says, 'Stilks, Sheena looks in pain. Maybe we should do something.'

Me and Nick both shouted at the same time, 'Ambulance!'

Then it was game on. Everyone started panicking at once.

Fortunately, the ambulance got there in double-quick time, and got Sheena to the hospital as quickly as they could which was fortunate 'cos she had the baby within 20 minutes of arriving there.

That was my first daughter, Emma.

So Sheena hadn't been messing about after all.

* * *

Back at the Station, it was getting more violent and I was getting edgy, I was really jumpy all the time.

I remember once I was on the door and this fella was looking at me. I thought, Right, then looked away. Then I looked back over and he made eye contact with me again. I thought, What the fuck's all this about? but I let it drop.

Later, I glance in his direction and there he is making bloody eye contact with me again. He's still standing there in the same place, hasn't moved for a fucking hour. Now I'm getting the hump. So I'm pacing up and down and I said to one of the other doormen, 'If that geezer don't stop staring at me, I'm gonna go over there and do the fucking cunt. I ain't having it.'

I look again and he's still staring at me. So I decided to psych meself up, flex up, and get on with it. He was quite a big geezer, short hair and a bit rough looking. So I went over.

'Right, mate, I've had enough of you fucking looking at me all night. If you want, it we'd better go outside and have it, have a fucking straight'ner.'

So he goes, 'Look, mate, I don't want any trouble.'

'Don't want no fucking trouble, you've been standing there looking at me for a fucking hour and a fucking bit.' I was getting really mad with him. 'Come on, outside, here we go.'

And he says, 'I'm sorry, mate, but I can't.'

'Whatcha mean, you can't.'

'I can't go outside. You see I ain't got no legs. I lost them at the Falklands. I came here with me mates – there they are over there dancing – and they just put me here. I can't move until they come back.'

Well, you can imagine how I felt, fucking humbled I was. So I apologise to him and all that and back off. But that was when I first realised the level of violence was not just escalating, but it was starting to get to me as well. You have to be on your toes in my game 'cos it can go off at any time, but now I was wondering if I was starting to imagine it as well.

I was head doorman and doing well. Lots of other places were asking me to help 'em get bouncers for the doors. Everything was on the up, but there was a nagging doubt at the back of my mind, making me unsure of meself. What if, one day, I couldn't fucking handle it. Bollocks to that, I thought. If you get those doubts there's only one thing to do – go in harder.

As things got rougher at the Station, more and more blood was starting to get spilled which inevitably would splash all over our jackets. And if the police turned up during one of the brawls outside, you'd be in for a right questioning and maybe get nicked if they saw all the blood on your fucking clothing. This was when we had the idea of swapping the bloody jackets with the bouncers inside who were wearing clean ones. After a particularly nasty fight, you'd have to run inside and swap your jacket before the Old Bill arrived.

One night, a load of black guys turned up at the door and I said, 'Look, lads, you can't come in.'

'Why not?'

''Cos you got the wrong fucking coloured shoes on.'

We'd had a lot of trouble with these lads and the manager didn't want 'em in.

One of 'em said, 'Well, that ain't a good enough reason.'

I said, 'It's fucking good enough for me, mate. You ain't coming in … wrong coloured shoes … fuck off!'

So one of them kicks me in the leg and runs off with his mate. I thought, I ain't having none of this, so I grab this bottle and go running up the road chasing him. I was just going to belt him one when this police car pulls up next to me and asks what's going on.

I said, 'Officer, this guy has just tried to glass me with this bottle and I've taken it off him.'

'Right, well, do you want to press charges?'

'Not really, I'm all right.'

The Old Bill went away and the next thing I know the guys have come back with their mates. They parked a red van outside the pub and loads of the fuckers started piling out tooled up with pick-axe handles, car jacks, metal bars, sticks, anything they could find.

But they couldn't get at us straight away because of some railings that are outside the front of the Station so they lost the element of surpise. So we steamed in first. We were hitting them, they were hitting us and it looked like we were winning because they moved over to the other side of the road where the Plough pub was. They were trying to get away. But we caught up with them.

I put a steel-capped boot into one of them, while another one tries to get me round the throat, but I shrug the cunt off. Now everybody's fighting in the middle of the road. Complete fucking mayhem. Then I hear the siren. Some bastard had called the police.

Quickly we retreat back into the Station and change jackets. No blood on us anywhere. But the police wouldn't believe we hadn't been involved in a fight. They were puzzled but they knew something had been going on, especially as the blacks on the other side of the road looked as though they had been through a world war. Anyway, there were no arrests that night, but the following morning the manager had a call asking all the doormen to go down to the police station.

I say to the manager, 'I ain't fucking going, Tom. If they want to interview me, they can fucking well come down here.'

All the other doormen turned themselves in, but I refused. They got charged and in the end the case went to Crown Court. But it was thrown out because the police lost some of the statements and the court decided that because the geezers had come tooled up they must have been the aggressors. To me, it was just another night on the door, another incident. Don't know why the Old Bill thought it was anything unusual.

They had to take the blokes to court because race had become a big issue round those parts then. If the police hadn't done anything, they would have been accused of not caring 'cos it was only a load of black guys. But, to me, it was just trouble that had to be sorted out. In those days, if things went off you just had to go in and worry about the politics of it all later.

The Station was just a pub but, as Whitbread's first type of themed venue pub, it attracted a lot of kids. Ecstasy had just come out then and they were taking a lot of Es, there wasn't a lot of Charlie around but Es were everywhere. They were all on that and drink and were just fucking stupid.

One night I was clearin' 'em all out. 'Can you go now, lads, can you go now?' But two of them stayed at the bar. The licensing officer came in to make sure we were getting them out on time and I explained we'd nearly got 'em all out except for the bastards at the bar who were refusing to move. They were sitting there laughing at me, thinking I couldn't do fuck all while the licensing guy was there.

But when he had gone, I went up to the blokes and said, 'Now you're gonna go ...' and with that – *bang*! – but I hadn't hit him. It was one of my mates who'd hit him. The bloke went running out and told the licensing officer who came in, pointed at me and said, 'Was that the guy who hit you?'

'Yes, I think so, or maybe not.'

So the licensing officer comes up close to me and says, 'Stilks, I know you've hit him, or got someone to hit him, but for fuck's sake will you slow up?'

But I had no intention of doing that, especially when I spotted three of the guys I had thrown out fighting in the middle of the road between the Station and the Plough.

There was this fucking idiot beating up this kid. So I picked up a glass and ran over and smashed it over his head. That started it. Other idiots from the Plough side came storming into the road wanting to beat us up as well. It was a complete free-for-all.

There were taunts, shouts, it was all kicking off. 'Yeah, you cunt, come and get some of this …' There was no time for changing jackets now.

The licensing officer must have phoned the police because they came in three or four van-loads and they got lost in the mayhem that was going on.

'Stilks, you've gone over the top this time, you've started a near riot out there,' says one of them.

'It was nothing to do with us,' I say. 'We came out of the pub to help you lot. You were the ones that were in trouble.'

But the incident was never forgotten by the yobs over at the Plough who would continue to taunt us. Then, one sunny day, when they were drinking outside, I snapped. I just said to 'em, 'You happy, eh, you happy?'

So they started throwing their glasses over the road at the Station. One goes through the window. Next comes a bottle aimed at me. I dodge it. The other doormen came running out to try and drag me back inside the pub, but I hadn't finished talking to the yobs.

I started shouting, 'Go on, smash the pub up if you like, I don't live here. I only fucking work here, you silly bastards.'

I was ranting and screaming at them as salvo after salvo of bottles and glasses were raining down. There was broken glass everywhere. The doormen were screaming at me, 'For fuck's sake, Stilks, get back in here you'll get yourself killed.'

'I ain't finished lecturing these cunts yet,' I replied. 'Come on, ya scum bastards, come and fight.'

But they wouldn't – all they could do was throw more bottles. It was fucking hailing glass, but I didn't give a shit.

'Come on, ya cunts. Smash the fucking street up … I don't give two shits. I don't fucking live here – you fucking lot do.'

And then I turned on my heel and walked slowly from the centre of the road to the Station.

Just as I got to the door, I looked back at the braying mob of drunken louts, pulled myself up to my full height, lifted my arms high into the air, and shouted at them, 'I HAVE NO FUCKING INTENTION OF SLOWING UP.'

5

MUTINY!

GIVE EVERYONE THE SAME RESPECT THEY GIVE YOU.
STILKS

THERE'S ALWAYS ONE FUCKING IDIOT WHO THINKS THEY'RE A HARD BASTARD AND THEY BELIEVE THE WAY THEY CAN PROVE IT IS BY STANDING UP TO STILKS. IT'S HAPPENED TO ME SO MANY TIMES OVER THE YEARS I'VE LOST COUNT. BUT AFTER I'D RANTED AT THE YOBS FROM OVER THE PLOUGH, IT BECAME OPEN SEASON TO SEE WHICH ONE OF THEM COULD BRING ME DOWN.

I was on the door with Joe one Wednesday, there were just the two of us, when he turns and says to me, 'Stilks, you know that fella you told to fuck off about half-an-hour ago … he's come back with a pick-axe handle.'

I thought to meself, Where the fuck do they keep getting all these pick-axe handles from?

So he's waving it about outside and shouting, 'Come out here, Stilks, come out here.' So I went out and recognised him as one of the local idiots who was a regular at the Plough and a fucking nutcase.

I told Joe to go inside while I sorted it. I told the geezer, 'Put that pick-axe handle down and me and you'll have a straight'ner, then you can fuck off.'

He says, 'No, I'm gonna do you with this.'

'Nah, put it down and fight me straight.'

He put the handle down and came over to the door. I said, 'Go on, do your best.' I'd put on a little weight and I was confident I wasn't going to lose. With that, he comes up and hits me in the stomach – *whack!* – and then goes for my throat and tries to strangle me. Now all the people in the pub start comin' out to see what's happening. 'Stilks is losing' is the whisper goin' round. So I look down at the guy whose tryin' to have a go at me. He's only a short bloke, about 10-11st and I said to him, 'Have you finished yet? Right, because now it's my turn.'

And with that I pushed him in the chest 'til he was up against the wall and punched him twice in the stomach, pulled him down, hit him in the face with me knee, threw him to the floor, and then kicked him in the head into the railings outside the pub.

I looked at Joe and said, 'That's how you deal with 'em'.

I'd been at the Station about seven years by then and the décor in the pub was beginning to look a bit rough. So it was decided they were going to re-fit it. But they didn't want to lose me because I'd been there right from the beginning, so they said there was a pub round the corner called the

Camden which was getting a bit of trouble and would I go and help them out for a few months, and then I'd get me job back.

Of course I would; it was only four roads from where I lived. Nice one. So I went and introduced meself to the landlord, bloke named Dougie.

'Get much of it round here?' I asked.

'Nah, not much trouble really. Bit recently, but fuck all else.'

It looked as if it was run decently so I said I'd give it a try seven nights a week, same money as I was getting at the Station. Anyway, at the end of the night there was no trouble, so I said to Dougie, 'Look, you ain't got no trouble here. I'm only three minutes' walk up the road so I'll tell you what I'm gonna do … I'm not gonna come in Monday to fucking Friday. I'm just gonna come in Friday night for about an hour to chuck 'em out and pick up me money. How about that?

He looked at me open-mouthed.

'But, Dougie mate,' I continued, 'if you ever get any trouble in this pub, I want you to phone me at home, and I'll come down straight away and sort it out. Right?'

I'm standing there a bit menacing, telling him exactly what game I'll be playing and he suddenly finds his tongue and says, 'Yeah, yeah, good idea, if that's what you want to do, Stilks, yeah.'

Fucking good idea, I thought to meself, it's fucking brilliant.

115

So I went home and told Sheena about the set-up. 'Listen, love,' I said, 'there's a guv'nor down the road named Dougie. If he ever phones, just tell him that I'm not in. I'm never in, right, got it?'

It worked a bloody treat. I went in there for an hour every Friday and he gave me a week's wages and then when the Station re-opened, I went back there – and Dougie still kept on paying me.

Of course, it went off once at the Camden, when this cocky little bastard walked in. He was a nuisance, a little shit, probably taken drugs or summat. So Dougie barred him, got the usual verbal, then the bloke's gone and left. Dougie phones Sheena, who says she ain't seen me. He's starting to panic … that's when I walk in the pub.

'Where the fuck you been, Stilks? Summat's gonna go off and you're supposed to be fucking covering me.'

'Stay calm, Dougie, stay fucking calm. I'm here, I sensed it mate, I sensed it.'

Sure enough, the geezer comes back and I say, 'Hold it. You're barred. You know it and I know it so you're not coming in.'

He goes away, but I haven't seen the last of the bastard because after the pub's shut he comes back with these milk bottles. I take one look and think, Jesus. The things were full of fucking petrol!

One of them smashes through the window and it erupts. *Smash!* Another hits the front woodwork and it's on fire. We were being bloody fire-bombed.

The curtains are on fire, the woodwork is burning and this little shit legs it up the road. Dougie's going mad, running around with buckets of water, trying to douse the flames, and as the guy had already scarpered I decided to help Dougie try and put out the fire. Fortunately, the brigade got there in double-quick time and prevented what could have turned into a really nasty incident.

As for the geezer who did it, he got caught 'cos the bloke at the petrol station where he had been filling the milk bottles had enough savvy to phone the cops and give 'em the number of his car. The little shit got put away for four years and fucking good riddance to him.

'I thought you was supposed to prevent this sort of thing happening,' says Dougie, turnin' on me.

'Come on, mate … I might be Mr Stilks but I ain't fucking Asbestos Man.' Anyway, that was the end of me at the Camden, so I went back to the re-vamped Station for good.

It looked really shiny, really posh, they had done it wonderful and I thought, It's going to be great working here now. None of your rough crowd any more. This was like a real bit of the West End come down to Welling.

That was when I spotted this guy at the bar having a piss. He would have been welcome down the Camden the other day, but I wasn't havin' none of it at the new-look Station. There he was swayin' against the bar and, as he sees me, he pulls himself up and starts to get fucking taller and taller. I'm thinking, Fuckin' hell, and says to him, 'Whatcha think you're doin'? You're goin', mate, you're pissed, you're

pissin' up against the bar, you dirty cunt. Right, come on.'
And then I start dragging him out.

He's pissed, he's swayin', he's a big 'un and I realise I've
got to knock him out with one blow straight away. The
barmaids have seen what he's been doin' and so has the
landlord. So I have to be seen taking control. I've got him
outside.

'You know what you've done wrong,' I say.

'No, Stilks, it ain't nuthin' like that.'

'You pissed up against the bar and now you've gotta go
down.'

So I line him up and, *bang*! I've swung it. But he was so
bloody pissed he swayed and dodged my right. I'd missed. I
thought, Christ, if he keeps his wits, he can kill me. So I
shouted at him, 'Right, now fucking behave yourself. I'm just
showing you what I could have done if I wanted. I'm letting
you off, so fuck off.' He settled for a telling off.

By this time, I was getting well known in the doorman
world and people would ask for me specifically because they
wanted a face – someone who was known and who the
punters would fear. I fitted the bill perfectly and offers
started coming in.

The guv'nor at the King's Lodge (a nightclub in West
Kingsdown) Terry Rich wanted a new head doorman 'cos
there were loads of gyppos up there, loads of trouble. And
he wanted someone who was known, someone who could
stop things before they went off. He wanted a face and he
was willing to pay. But I wanted it both ways. The King's

Lodge didn't close till 2.00am, so I could finish at the Station at 11.00pm and piss off up there.

This was at the time that the raves had just started and every fucker was out their head. Mick Brown, from Capital Radio, was there at the time trying to promote the place. He was there for eight weeks on a contract advertising the place. I was quite friendly with Mick and everybody used to call me Top Man at that time. So as a joke I told him he wouldn't be allowed in the Lodge unless he played a record on his Sunday show at Capital and dedicated it to 'Stilks, Top Man at King's Lodge'. This went on for weeks and we were getting recognised but when it came to the bleedin' music at the Lodge, Mick was relying too much on club stuff and it wasn't working.

I said to the guv'nor, 'That's fuckin' shit. Kids want house music and rap.'

'Nah, you don't know what you're talking about, Stilks, this ain't the bloody West End, mate. We're in the middle of fucking nowhere.'

'Right, you useless prat, I'll tell you what we'll do. Let me put the money up for advertising, right, and I'll take the money on the door and you can have the money behind the bar. And, OK, I'll pay for the bleedin' doormen. Deal?'

So I put all my men up there and took over the door. I started givin' it a go and I called the night The Slam. It was a success and from there I started doing the Bank Holiday all-nighters. I had four men on the door which later went up to six and I was paying for the DJ who was a fella named

Paul Docherty, the Doctor of Music, and he pulled a big fucking crowd. I soon sussed out over the weeks that the way to get 'em in was to have more than one or two DJs, with a load of 'em all doing a half-hour each. They all brought their own crowd and so I always had a full club. It was about a fiver to get in in those days and I was taking the bloody lot, but I wasn't making that much of a profit – oh, all right then, I was.

So it all took off from there. One of the weight-lifters I was training down at the gym, who later became a British champion, was also puttin' on a few little dos here and there so I grabbed him and I said, 'You're now my partner. Gorrit?'

We started putting on nights at an old wine cellar in Woolwich and my new partner would run it.

So by now I'm running the King's Lodge as head doorman, I'm still head doorman at the Station, I'm head doorman down at the Wine Cellar in Woolwich, and I've got the gym. Enough to keep any fucker busy, you might think. Well, bollocks, 'cos that's when I started me own record label.

This kid, Matt Grey, comes up to me while I'm at the King's Lodge and he goes, 'I make records – at home.'

'Yeah, so fucking what?'

'I'm looking for a backer.'

'To do what?'

'So I can go to a studio and make an acetate and then make records and sell 'em to specialist shops.'

'Yeah, and how am I gonna make fucking money then?

'Well, I make the music and we go 50-50.'

At the time, I was making money everywhere and all he wanted was £2,000 to get started. I was still a partner with Peter Hayford down the gym, so I suggested to Peter we went a grand each and tried this lad out. This kid had just broken away from the group Orbital, named after the M25. He was one of the main men behind it but didn't want to be recognised because at the time it was hot putting out records but nobody knew who was doin' 'em.

First of all, we just knocked out white label records with no information on 'em. I went round all the small record shops and I was givin' 'em 50 records at a time. I'd go back a week later, get me money and leave 'em more.

We released six records, including one called 'The Slam' after the nights I put on at the King's Lodge and that got on to a compilation album. I never got any fucking money for that – so if you're reading this, mate, I'm coming after ya. Beware.

In the end, it was fucking success that beat me. I only had that one guy making music. We went 50-50 and I'm a fair man. If we have a deal, we have a deal and I ain't gonna rip you off. Eventually, he had enough money to go out on his own and didn't need anyone to put up more money.

I didn't look for another bloke to make records with because I'd got the gym, I'd got property, I'm training Olympic lifters, and I'm head doorman at three places. I had no intention of slowing down but this was getting fucking ridiculous.

One night, I needed Peter Hayford, my partner at the gym, to work the door with me down the Lodge and, of course, it's that night it all kicks off. They were all gyppos, and they were all from the same bleedin' family or summat. The whole place was in uproar. Glasses were being thrown round the club and I'm thinkin', Fuckin' hell … what's happenin'? I said to Peter, 'Let's go.' I wanted to be there first, I didn't want to let anyone think I was frightened or I couldn't do the job. Most head doormen send their men in first before they bother, but with me it was the other way round. I lead from the front. I rushed in, knocked people over, fucking drinks flyin' everywhere. I used to cause more fights getting to the fucking fight!

Peter and I were there in the thick of it, standing back to back as glasses were hurlin' round about us. This geezer hits me straight on the chin and I've fallen back and I'm sitting on me arse after crashing into this fuckin' fella behind me. I've looked back – it's Peter. He's on the floor as well. I've looked and laughed. 'This is good, innit?' I shouted at him. Now all the gyppos were going for a kicking match at us. So as one of 'em aimed, I grabbed his leg and he was down on the floor with us. Now it was really getting good. I'd yank 'em down and Peter would hit 'em. Next one please.

Peter was my best friend. In fact, he was more than that, he was the brother I had always craved when I was growing up. My sisters Yianoula and Maria were fine, but they had had a Greek Orthodox upbringing and were treated differently from me by my mum and dad. I was the eldest male and what I always bleedin' craved was a brother who I could relate to and talk to and all that bollocks. So when I made a mate, I made a mate for fucking life. And with Peter it was just that. Not only had he coughed up the dosh to help set up PecS Gym, but he'd also been with me setting up the record label – a diamond geezer. Now here we were on the floor of the Lodge together battling it out with the shit yobbos. I couldn't have wanted any other bloke with me in a situation like that. I thought I had been bloody blessed to know such a mate.

I thoroughly enjoyed that night. Everybody was getting' hit an fallin' over, but nobody was hurt that much. When things kick off, you have to go in fast. If you hang around thinkin' 'Shall I or shan't I?' then you've fuckin' blown it. You'll start getting twitchy and worryin' about whether you're gonna get hurt, whether you might end up doin' ten years … you think too much. And that ain't good for ya.

The first rule for any good bouncer is to get over there and get stuck in and don't think about it. I never, ever think about my own safety. I always think about the safety of others, the safety of people in the club. Get into the situation fast and you get a great adrenalin rush. The thrill about hittin' someone in my game is that you're putting someone right. They shouldn't have been doing what they were doing in the first place.

The idea is to make the guv'nor of the club feel safe. He has to feel he's got the right bloke for the job and the only way to do that is for the head doorman to have full control of the club. When I'm in full control, incidents don't go off that much. It's as if everyone knows that someone is there in control. And it's that aura of control that marks out a fucking good bouncer. Once I have control, I can do what I like in that club. I don't have to stand on the door and say, 'Sorry, mate, you've got jeans and trainers on.' I have other blokes to do that. I can usually just sit at the bar and observe what's goin' on. And once the word gets round that Stilks is at the bar, there isn't any trouble. That's the kind of control it takes years to learn and build up. But it is because I have that control that I've become top of my profession. I'm not just there to keep people out of the club or pub, but I'm there to make sure no one makes an arsehole of themselves while they're inside as well.

Most incidents will start over pissed blokes trying to pick up girls or spilling drinks and it's not often you can spot the bleedin' troublemakers on the way in. At the door, they'll be well dressed, calm and placid.

One night, I'd got it all under control at the King's Lodge, everythin' was going sweet, no aggro. In fact, it had been like that for about nine months, and that's a worry. 'Cos once things go really quiet, they start cutting down on the doormen or, even worse, payin' less money.

So I was pleased when the gyppos outside started playing up. Four of us ran out there and Terry, the guv'nor at the Lodge, shut the door behind us to stop any scum gettin' in. He thought we were having it off with the gyppos but, in fact, it didn't develop into anything at all. So I thought, I know what I'm going to do, and ran round the back where there's the fridge full of steaks and burgers and all that bollocks. I grabbed one of the steaks and slapped it on me chest. I went back round the front where there wasn't even a bloody scuffle by now and shouted, 'It's OK, Terry, you can open the door now, mate, it's all over.'

He opens it a little and peeps out. 'Come in, come in,' he says. 'What's happened to you?'

'Fuckin' hell, Terry, it was fuckin' awful out there. Them gyppos had a whole load of tools, everything. Look, I've got one of the fuckin' cunt's blood all over me.'

'Christ, come and sit down. I'd better make you a cup of tea to calm you down.'

'That'd be very nice, Terry. Thanks.'

'That's OK. I always thought that lot would be big trouble. I think we'd better beef up the door a bit for the next few weeks.'

'Good idea, Terry, good fucking idea, mate.'

There were loads of little scams like that you had to work to keep your job. The toilets were always a good 'un. Every now and then, you'd go an' smash 'em up a bit and make out a load of fuckin' hooligans had been doin' it. Or we'd even get blokes to smash it up for us just to keep our jobs going. One thing I must say about the bloody Lodge, though … there was no way you could nick any money. Terry was really fast on the money, never left it lying about.

At the time, I was also looking after a pub in Erith and I had about four of me doormen on there. One of them, Jack, beat up a bloke down there and the bloke he hit was a bit of a face.

So these guys came up to me at the Station and say, 'Do you know the doormen down in Erith?'

'Yeah, course, they're part of my team.' That was the stupidest thing I ever said.

One of the geezers pulls out this shooter and says, 'Right, well one of 'em beat up the wrong guy.' He starts wavin' the gun at me. 'Well, you're gonna have to tell us who he is.'

'Look, I'm part of a big team. They all work for me. And as for your fucking gun, you can put that away, because it ain't happenin' and I ain't gonna give you the name of the person you're looking for. So why don't ya walk away?'

By this time I was fuckin' shitting meself.

'If you want to, you can go down there and try and sort it out for yourself, but I'm tellin' ya there's a lot of us.'

At the time, these blokes were going around trying to frighten a lot of people. They were trying to take over the south-east patch by threats. The firm was small then, but now it's pretty big and the guy who runs it is an absolute nutter. But I never really had any trouble because I was well respected. They never tried to come along and muscle in on the fucking doorman game and, in fact, I became quite friendly with some of the biggest firms who used to come and drink in the Station. So nothing could happen.

If I wanted to, I could have taken over this side of Kent if I had decided to get involved with drugs and extortion and that sort of thing. I have been approached to get into the big league but I am too smart. I didn't want the fucking risk of getting put away for 10 or 15 years when I could earn the money legally by using me head.

Some people look at gangsterism as quick money and can't do bugger all else. I did once become an enforcer for a guy who died in Thamesmead but that was much later on and I don't like talking about that. We did get approached by firms but they were really just 'testers'. They were testing you to see how hard you were and how far you would go. And once they could see I wasn't up for it, wasn't gonna let 'em muscle in, they started treating me with respect.

This big fella came up once and started talking and proddin' me and, well, that fucks me off. I don't like people in my space touchin' me while they're talking. I really hate that.

So I said, 'Do me a favour. Fuck off. Talk to me, don't touch me.' And the bastard touches me again, so with that I push him off and tell him, 'Fuck off.' It was only later I found out he was connected to Reg Parker's firm, a right hard bastard he is. But he's a friend of mine. I'd been on the doors so long I was fuckin' connected to everybody. Anyway, the bloke I pushed goes up to Reg and says he wants me done over because I'd disrespected him in front of everybody, and he was a name.

The following week, the bloke comes back to the club.

'Yeah, what the fuck do you want,' I say.

'Reg has sent me down to apologise to you.'

'Yeah, and why's that?'

'I told him what happened last week and he said if I didn't come down and apologise *he* was going to beat me up.'

Reg had told him that if I'd told him off or hit him then I'd done it for a reason and he was to apologise.

I was never brought up with gangsters or the underworld, as you know by now, but where I operated was where they used to have their fun. Remember, only mugs and thugs drink at clubs. You don't get your city people coming down to the pubs and clubs on the outskirts of Kent for a drink, you get fuckin' idiots that come out and wanna have late drinks. So that's how I started meeting a lot of strange people and a lot of the gangsters were some of the most honest people I've ever met. Men of their word. I've met a lot of hard people – straight people – who have said things to me but never come up with the goods. They are the liars. A good gangster has to be a man of his word or he's in big trouble; without that, he ain't got anything.

To be a gangster, you don't have to be hard. To pull a trigger or rob a bank or sell drugs doesn't take a lot of muscle. The enforcer is always a lot harder than the villain. And I'm hard. Yeah, they can come back and shoot me, but that's only if you take liberties and I don't. I don't take liberties with the villains or with the geezers who work for me. I'd built up my empire of clubs and pubs round the south-east and all the blokes on the doors were really guys I'd recruited from the gym, people like Peter Hayford and the rest. And they respected me and I respected them. That's the way it works, on respect and trust. So if any firm wanted to try and take me over or work my patch, then all of us doormen would hang together. That way, nobody dared try, not even after I'd been threatened over the incident down at Erith when Jack beat up one of the faces.

I could call on 30 of the hardest bastards around and they were totally loyal. Once people knew that, they didn't fuck with me.

I was never interested in the gangster scene, 'cos I was interested in money, not glory for fuck all. I was in it for perks, which everybody does in any game. A steady supply of cash was more important to me than a ten or £20,000 heist. Yes, I've mixed with the underworld, but one thing has kept me in good stead with 'em. I can always remember a face, but I'm no fucking good at names. And that's how it should be, because if anyone tries to get information out of me, they can't – I can't remember names.

* * *

But there's one name I'll never fucking forget.

He was the brother I never had, my right-hand man, my business partner ... and he turned out to be a cunt.

I was runnin' all these fuckin' doors and the pressure was on me. I've got doormen everywhere and I'm being driven fucking mad. I'd be swapping doormen around, giving them nights off when it was slack, but generally trying to keep 'em employed. But, of course, every now and again someone had to take a bleedin' night off, there wasn't enough work for everybody. I was tryin' to treat 'em all properly and fairly because they were all friends of mine as well as being doormen.

Naturally, some of them weren't too happy with the situation and they wanted it changed. They wanted to be head doormen of their own pubs or clubs and not be part of Stilks' team any more. They wanted to take over. My right-hand man was Peter. I'd looked after him and he had half of the fucking records, half of the gym and half of everything else. I trusted him. I had to, 'cos I was running too much to keep an eye on everything meself.

I got a whiff of all the squabbling that was going when one of me doormen came up to me at the Station.

'Is that right then, Stilks?' he says.

'What's right? What's wrong? Come on.'

'That, like, the firm might be splittin' up, an' that.'

'Where you get that idea from?'

'Just, like, thought I'd let you know.'

'So it's a fuckin' mutiny is it? And who's behind all this bollocks then?'

'I dunno, Stilks, really I dunno. Just a whisper you know, thought I'd let ya know.'

It was no use beating the geezer up. He'd never cough who was behind it all. Doormen are tough and the first rule is, ya never grass. Nah, I'd have to sort this one out for meself, even if it meant taking the fucking lot of them on.

But then I thought, Shit, some of these blokes were giants, they were 20-fuckin'-stoners, big cunts, stronger than me. So

I was thinking, How do I beat 'em? If I stood there toe-to-toe, I might beat one, but if I fought another one after that, he might beat me. So I thought back to the old bullying days at school and realised that bullies fight in packs, they can't fight on their own. So what I had to find out was when was their most vulnerable time – and that was, like most people, at four o'clock in the mornin', when the bastards were in bed.

So at 4.00am I'd go round the houses, knock on the door, and tell 'em, 'Come out, I've heard you wanna take over this, take over that, and I'm not fuckin' havin' it. Come out here now and fight me.'

Remember, I don't even drink or smoke.

Of course, they wouldn't come out; they were naked and didn't even have any shoes on. And even if they did, I was going to win 'cos it was a one-to-one fight and I had big steel toe-capped boots on. You don't go against that if you're bollock naked. And they had no back-up. Remember, by this time I had really lost my temper with these fucking blokes. I'd set 'em up with jobs and they were ready to shit on me behind my back.

After harassing about three of 'em round their houses in the middle of the night, they got the message.

'Come out, you bastard,' I'd scream. 'I have no fucking intention of slowing up.'

Eventually, they all backed off and the rebellion fizzled out.

But I was really pissed off with Peter Hayford because he should have sorted out the problem for me before it went too far. He should have come and told me what was happenin' within the firm. But no one told me. In fact, I found out that Peter had instigated the whole thing. He was stirring it up with my men so he could grab a bigger piece of the bleedin' action himself. What a tosser!

So I went round to his house and knocked on the door one Sunday afternoon.

'Peter, I wanna have a word with ya.'

'What's that about, Stilks?'

'Have we fucking fallen out?'

'Nah, Stilks.'

'I think we have. You've been sayin' and doin' things behind me back which you know ain't true. You're trying to fucking split up the firm and take over. And it's no use fucking denying it. I've spoken to the other blokes and I think you've been manipulative and rude, Peter. That's what I fucking think.'

His daughter Emma comes down the stairs so I get a pound out of me pocket and say, 'Emma, do me a favour, love, go up the sweet shop a minute. I want to talk to your dad.'

That's when I saw Peter physically tremble. His wife was in the kitchen but I said, 'Right, Peter, you and me are going to have a straight'ner. Outside.'

He's about 17–18st and I'm about 14, but he still says, 'Nah, we don't have to do that,' and then he throws a fast right, and he misses, but his weight has thrown me on to the settee. I'm on the settee with him on top of me and his hand on my face, but I'm quite happy with the situation because in judo one of my best areas is ground work, so I'm comfortable. He starts putting pressure on my face and I'm thinking, Lovely, this ain't a problem. He thinks he's winning but I've got one of his fucking arms and I've packed it under mine.

Then I open my mouth as wide as I can and I'm waiting there like a frog and I know sooner or later his hand is going to slip into my mouth. I know it and I'm waiting for it.

His hand goes into my mouth and he's tugging, pullin' at my jaw. He thinks he's got it, thinks he's wrenching my jaw to pieces when *snap*! My teeth come down. I've got him and I can feel one of the fingers. It's gone between the knuckle, it's gone through the skin and through into the fucking joint. I've got it and he's squealing like a pig.

Then he starts shouting, 'Yank, Yank, help me, help me. Yank!' And bounding up comes this American pit bull-terrier barking like mad. But the dog can't work it out.

Peter's shouting, 'Let go, let go.'

The blood's coming down my face and drippin' on to my shirt. But I love it 'cos I've got him, I know I've done him.

He's screaming for Yank to help him, his wife has come in from the kitchen and is hysterical and crying. I thought, Any minute now that kid's gonna come back from the sweet shop. I knew I'd have to try and finish it as quick as possible. So I start hitting him in the face with lots of lefts and rights. He's begging me to stop but why should I? Instead, with his hand in me mouth, I start walking round the house with him. By now, all the blood is going up the walls and round the furniture. I thought, Don't think much of his chances when he's in that line at Casualty. Bloody National Health Service.

Everywhere it was. For good measure, I went *smack*! and gave him one on the nose. There was more blood now.

But Peter managed to open the front door and the first thing that happened was the bloody pit bull shot out there like a fucking bullet and ran down the road at top speed. It was a right wanker of a dog. Peter had got the dog to make himself look hard but, when the chips were down, the dog was no fucking use at all.

Did you know that a human bite is far worse than a dog bite? No wonder the cunt of a hound scarpered. He was up against Stilks.

Anyway, as I left the house, I shouted at Peter, 'I'll be back, I haven't had enough. It'll carry on, this.'

But it didn't. Peter went up the hospital 'cos his hand had swollen to the size of a fucking balloon. He knew he was beaten and he phoned me later and said he didn't want no more and all that bollocks, and that was it. We have never been friends again.

Before I put the phone down, I laid it on the line to him. 'I'm the one that's really hurt, Peter, your fucking hand will heal. When I make friends, I expect them to be friends for life. But you betrayed me, you let me down. You've shown me how fuckin' shallow and greedy people can get. But beware, Peter, you're gonna have to be on your guard for ever.' And with that I slammed the phone down and stood there in front of the hall mirror looking at my reflection and seething.

Peter went down the gym later and told the blokes I'd smashed him up for no reason and they thought I was fucking well out of order. Well, they could think what the fuck they wanted. They'd been easily led by the bastard, they could think what they liked.

The firm was finished. Now it was a question of who could survive.

6

RAISING THE STAKES

**NO ONE GIVES YOU RESPECT,
YOU HAVE TO EARN IT.**
STILKS

137

IT WAS ALL OVER. THEY HAD BETRAYED THE ONE THING IN LIFE THAT IS ABOVE EVERYTHING ELSE. THEY'D BETRAYED TRUST. I SAID TO THE BOYS, 'I'VE HAD ENOUGH. YOU ALL FUCK OFF AND DO YOUR OWN WORK.'

Some of them went over with Peter, some of 'em just drifted away. Me, I'd had enough of the fuckin' Lodge anyway.

After Peter, I felt I could never trust anybody. I was really let down. I'd thought that friendship came before fucking money and I thought we were a close-knit firm. We all trusted each other and what we'd done, we kept between ourselves. But obviously that wasn't the way. Some blokes did take my side and a few of them took Peter's. They later came to realise what a wanker he was and came back over to me, but that was years later. At the time, the damage had been done.

I shut down me nights at the King's Lodge, me all-nighters, and I shut down me raves at Woolwich. I'd had enough. They could all fuck off and I was gonna look after myself. A few of 'em never got any jobs after that; obviously, they weren't good enough to be doormen without me on their back all the time. Others found a bit of work here and there, but they were never successful doormen, full-time and in demand.

I didn't need a lot of money. As long as the bills were being paid at home, my life didn't revolve around earning loads of money. That was lucky, as the opportunities were drying up. The lease at the Lodge was up and Terry, who ran the place, was doing everything he could to put another lease together. But, sadly, he died attempting it and that was the end of the King's Lodge. So I said to Sheena, 'That's it, luv, I ain't gonna do no more door work.'

'Oh yeah, I'll believe that when I see it!'

'Maybe, Sheen, maybe … but I'm gonna spend a lot more time on me hobby anyway. You see.'

And I did spend more time on it.

My hobby always has been and always will be … gambling.

Right from the moment at school when I used to set up private three-card brag games in an empty classroom, I have always been in love with cards and the roll of the dice. But I've always had to have a fucking edge, if you know what I mean. That's why they were *my* card schools at Bloomfield Secondary. I could dictate the pace. I used to gamble at home with me mates until the early hours when Sheena kicked 'em out. And I never thought there was anything better than spending a day in the betting office. You can keep your fuckin' visits to bleedin' stately homes and the like. A tour round the nearest William Hills was what I always looked forward to.

And so it was the same when I decided to get involved with greyhounds; I needed to have a little edge. I thought if I got in with the dog owners and trainers, I would get information and I'd win more money. So I thought, Right, I'll go down Crayford dog track and see what I can suss out. I asked to speak to the manager and he gave me the number of a local dog trainer, a bloke named John Gibbons.

Then I went to see me brother-in-law, Mark Wheeler, who's a bit clued up and good with finances. He's a bit of a gambler, too. In fact, he works as a bank manager now. Anyway, I knew Mark before I even knew Sheena, having met him in a bookie's in Woolwich which he used to use. It was in the old days when all the windows were half blacked-out, like you were goin' into some porn shop. When we were kids, it always seemed a strange and mysterious place. We'd try and jump up high enough just to see over the blacked-out bit. But we never made it. Later, when I was old enough to go in the bookie's, the first thing I noticed was that it was always really smoky and there were just a few papers on the wall with the races on 'em. You'd put your bet on by putting it in a box with iron bars on, then you'd push it in and they'd take the bet. You'd never even see the person behind the counter. Then there'd be a little radio on the wall in the corner of the room and everybody would stand around it listening to the commentary on the dogs or the horses. How things have changed.

So when I went to see Mark, I said, 'Look, mate, we've been gambling a long time, it's about time we got some information.'

He thought it was a good idea. 'So what do we do then, Stilks?'

'Simple, Mark, we buy our own dog.'

'Buy our own dog! How much does a flippin' dog cost?'

'I dunno, that's why I want you to come with me. You're supposed to be good with fuckin' money an' all that. I've got a dog trainer's name and address from the geezer at the track and we'll go down there on Sunday and see him.'

So me and Mark went to see this Gibbons bloke and I put my cards on the table straight away.

'We ain't never been in the dog game before, but we wanna buy a dog.'

'Why do want to buy a dog?' said John Gibbons.

''Cos we want inside information, does that happen?'

'Yeah.'

'Well, that's why we're here. Have you got a dog to sell?'

'As it happens I do. I've got this one here. It was bought for the Derby, it's a bit older and the owner doesn't want it any more because, and I'll tell ya the truth, he's bought better dogs. But this one does suit Crayford and you'll have a lotta fun with him. But I'll give you one word of advice. Don't ever get attached to these dogs, they are only running machines. Bear that in mind. They are not pets and through your lifetime you might own many dogs.'

So I thought, Fine, and we agreed to buy the dog. It was called Capital Cinema.

'How much?' I asked.

'You watch it run,' said Gibbons. 'And decide for yourselves.'

I thought, Wass his game? but I kept quiet. I later realised he had no idea how much we had to spend and if we did get involved in the dog game then we might be buying three or four from him in the future. In those days, every dog you had cost £160 a month to keep with a dog trainer. Me and Mark thought it over and decided to go for it, and arranged to go down the track the following Saturday and see if Capital Cinema was ready to run.

So I get me dad and me uncle and tell 'em to come and watch this dog run 'cos me and me brother-in-law are gonna buy the fuckin' thing and we'd been told by the dog trainer to get on it 'cos it was going to win.

There were a whole load of us down there that night and we looked in the paper and Capital Cinema was favourite in the betting. It was 6-4, it was in with a bleedin' chance, it had Trap 1, and it looked like it could win.

So we got down there early and there was another dog trainer there named Paul Thomsett. It was his first night. It was a right busy night but we were all pretty confident. The first race went to one of Thomsett's dogs – I thought nothin' about it. The second race went to Thomsett again – lucky

143

bleeder. And then the third race, Thomsett's again. I thought, Hold up, wass his game then? I looked down the card. This new trainer had one more runner and it was in the same race as Capital Cinema. Thomsett's dog was 4-1 and we were still favourite.

When it got to the time of the race, the bookies started marking the prices up and just about every fucker at the track rushed down and started betting on the new trainer's dog. They were ploughing bloody money on it. 7-2, 3-1, the odds were coming down, 5-2. The bookies were wiping and chalking like it was going out of fuckin' business.

We were going 6-4, 7-4, 5-2, and I'm starting to panic.

'Mark, shall we get on now?'

'No, wait.'

'Ours can't be in with a chance 'cos the price is going out.'

Mark says, 'Don't let the fucking price worry you. The dog doesn't know what the price is!'

I'm thinking, He's right, he's right, the dog doesn't know. A minute later, 'Shall I get on now, Mark?'

'No, wait.'

I was ready to put on about £1,500. That's why I'd brought the whole family down. The dog trainer told us it was gonna win, he'd tuned it up, he wanted me to buy the dog and so I was ready with the big bet. I'd given money to me dad, me uncle, me friends and now they were all waiting for the signal to go. When I go, they all go and we lump on, that was the idea. We all hit a different bookmaker and spread the money around.

Meanwhile, Thomsett's dog is being backed down and down as more money is pouring on it. Capital Cinema is being pushed further out and now we are 7-2 and no longer favourite.

Then Mark shouts, 'OK, everybody, get on now.'

There's a right bleedin' scramble as Dad, clutching a fistful of notes, heads for one bookie. Me uncle Everett shoots off to get another, while me mates take another couple and I waltz up to another fucker and slap a few hundred on. All the £1,500 is slumped on and we've nicked the price at 7-2. No wonder Mark was looking pleased with himself, because as soon as the cash hit the bookies Capital Cinema was back down to 5-2, although it still wasn't favourite.

Then the race was really on. The traps open and Thomsett's dog gets off to a flyer straight out in front. I thought, Oh God, we can't win now, and closed me eyes. But when I opened 'em, I thought, Fuckin' hell, our dog's a fuckin' railer. And there it was as close to the rail as if it had been stuck on with super glue. And it was closing on the opposition, edging nearer and nearer to the lead held by Thomsett's greyhound. Capital Cinema steered round the last bend without losing a bleedin' inch.

We were all shouting, with Dad screaming, 'COME ON CAPITAL THEATRE, COME ON.'

'Actually, it's Cinema, Dad. It's Cinema. Oh, never mind! COME ON YOU BASTARD, RUN.'

And as the line got nearer, Capital Cinema, the dog we knew was gonna be ours, edged in front to win.

I'd won about £5,000 and me brother-in-law had won about the same, so we went back and bought the dog.

'I told you he'd run a good race today,' said John Gibbons. 'Came in nicely round that last bend I thought. He loves Crayford, you know, loves Crayford. So what do you think?

'How much?' I said.

'I told you, make me an offer.'

So we wrangled for a bit and then it was agreed we could have Capital Cinema for £1,000 because it was a bit of an old dog.

'I hope you take cash,' I said, fishing in me trouser pocket.

Looking back, it makes you realise just what mugs me and Mark were in the early days. After being in the game for a while, we realised that payin' £1,000 for a three-year-old dog like Capital Cinema was like paying £2 for a Mars bar. We had paid well over the top, but we were philosophical about the whole thing and thought of it as an educational step that any mug buying a dog for the first time would go through. We also found out that the dog was known in the kennel as Big Bad Ben because it was 38kg in weight, looked like a bloody pony, and hated other dogs – even other greyhounds.

When we went out walking, no bugger came anywhere near us as the dog used to go fucking apeshit. They used to clear the kennel yard before getting him out of his box – this dog was a flaming lunatic.

So our early plan to get matey with the other owners was fucked by the fact that we couldn't get within 400 yards of them without the dog going mental. So I thought, Bollocks to that, and I sent Mark out walking the dog while I chatted to the other blokes.

But the dog became the family's pride and joy. We'd go down the kennels every Sunday and feed it cheese.

After the first win, though, we went through November and December without so much as a sniff; he didn't finish in the first three in any of the races. We were starting to believe this wasn't the fucking money-spinnin' deal we had first thought. Sure, we had access to some good information, but we also had access to the bad as well. Overall, we were bleedin' well losing. Every time the dog trainer told us to get on, we got on. But I'm a very impatient gambler. If I only ever gambled on information, then I would be a very rich man. But when I go to the dog track, I've gotta bet on every fuckin' race and anything that moves. If someone says, 'Look, there's two old boys goin' to the toilet there,' I'll have a bet on which one is gonna piss first.

It was worth the trainer's fees to get the information about the dog. That's why we bought the dog in the first place. But just because Gibbons told us Capital Cinema had a fuckin' chance one week and didn't have one the next, didn't mean he was always right. There were other trainers out there who were bringing their dogs up to scratch as well. But most of the time you could rely on Gibbons, good man he was. A trainer knows when a dog's well and when he ain't. He has a look at his shit to see whether it's runny, he makes sure the diet is good, gives it few good walks and builds him up during the week before a bloody good race. If he kept him in a kennel for a week and didn't fuckin' feed him good quality food, he ain't gonna run well. So we used to wait for the magic words from John Gibbons: 'The dog is well, he is trying tonight. If you want to have a go on him, tonight's the night.'

But Capital Cinema was on the track one day, coming round the bend ready to take up the race when he falls and rolls over. There was a bloody hole in the sand and he had mis-footed. We ran round the back after the race to see what had happened to the bloody stupid animal. And that was when Gibbons gave us the bad news.

'Sorry, fellas,' he said. 'He's injured, he's lame.'

Mark was really fuckin' upset. 'What we gonna do now, Stilks?' he asked.

'Listen, Mark, remember what John told us at the beginning. Don't ever get attached to these dogs, they are only running machines. There's only one thing for it – we'll have to have the dog put down.'

Mark went bloody mad. 'Nah, we can't do that,' he shouted. 'We've got to make him better. We've got to.'

Gibbons didn't think it was that good an idea but he didn't fuckin' well care because every week we were giving him money. 'Make him better,' we'd say as we handed over the dough. And this went on week after fucking week. But the bleedin' dog wasn't getting any better.

'Mark, this is bloody stupid. We're throwing away all the money Capital Cinema's earned for us. It's better to cut and run now,' I said to him. 'Put the dog down and we'll

1972 aged 14

1974 aged 16

1976 aged 18

1977 aged 19

1978 aged 20

1979 aged 21

1980 aged 22

1983 aged 25

1986 aged 28

1990 aged 32

1994 aged 36

1996 aged 38

The changing faces of Stilks – from young tearaway to unstoppable force…

Top left: Me at 18 months old – and still with attitude!

Top right: With my sisters Maria and Yianoulla in Margate, 1968.

Bottom: With my mum, dad and sisters, Christmas 1966.

◄ was one of the Hard Bastards in Kate Kray's bestselling book of the same name. These pictures were taken at the glamorous book launch, and show some of the hardest faces in the country. (*Top, left to right*) Cornish Mick, Me, Joe Pyle, Frasier Tranter, Roy Shaw and Big John. (*Middle*) Me with my good friend and hard bastard Reg Parker. (*Bottom*) With the one and only Roy 'Pretty Boy' Shaw.

Top, left to right: Paul, Glen, real-life London gangster and Kray associate Tony Lambrianou, and me – we were all extras in the box-office smash *Snatch*.

Bottom: All the boys together at Keith Price's wedding in 2000. (*Left to right*) Richard, me, Wynne, Lloyd, Glen, Dutchie, Leroy, Sid, Glen and Paul.

Inset: Me with Dave Courtney.

If you want to be a hard bastard, you've got to keep in shape. (*Top left*) This is me aged 23 in 1981, and (*top right*) in 1987 I ran the Maidstone half marathon in 1 hour 42 mins. (*Middle*) With my good friend Brian in a big arm competition in 1994; and (*bottom*) showing what I'm made of in the gym…

Top: With Mick 'Saracen' and Mick 'Cobra' Wilson.

Middle: In 2001 I spent some time living with travellers. I'm pictured here with Lenny and Ricky.

Bottom left: Me with Andy and Baines in 1980.

Bottom right: With Nick Netley in 1983.

Top left: The youngest ever mayor? With Emma, Don and Sheena in 1998.

Top right: Dave and Gary with me in 1991 at the Aversham Arms in New Cross.

Middle: The boys (and girls!) from PecS Gym, Christmas 1994.
(*Left to right*) Jack, Sheena, Diane, Andy, Dave, Scott and Andy.

Bottom: With Jacko in 1999.

Top: The regulars at Bodywise Gym, 1992.

Middle: With Matt, Dave and Kevin at Gary Fox's wedding in 1998.

Bottom: This is the greyhound that turned out to be a nice little earner for yours truly…

I was one of the select few who was invited to Charlie Bronson's wedding to the beautiful Saira. (*Top left*) With my wife Sheena; (*top right*) with Charlie Breaker; (*middle*) with Tony Lambrianou and Joe Pyle; (*bottom*) with Tony again, and Baz Allen.

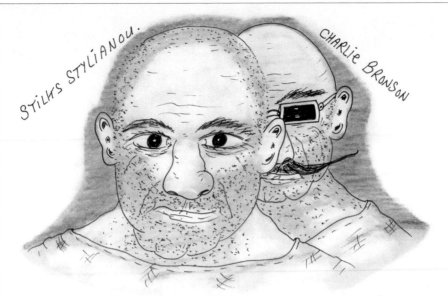

For Little Nikki.

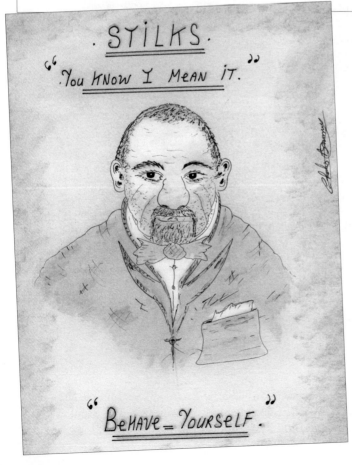

A selection of the drawings that Charlie Bronson has sent to me over the years…

" MY MOTHER'S APPLE-PIE
I CAN SMELL IT- IN MY HEAD.
BEAUTIFUL CRISPY PASTRY
I MAY AS WELL BE DEAD. "

The muscle we had on the door at The Station. With doormen like this, if you ain't got a ticket, you ain't coming in… (*Top*) With Lawrence and Joe; (*bottom left*) Tony and Keith Price; (*bottom right*) Lindon, Mark and Dave.

More muscle. (*Top*) At Saharas with Glen, Keith, Sid and Paul. (*Middle*) At the King's Lodge with Jim, Max and Peter. (*Bottom*) Dave, George and Dave at Stars.

Top left and right: At my wonderful wedding to Sheena in 1983. The Greek tradition is to have money pinned to your clothes…

Bottom left: In Cyprus with Katy, Sheena, Louise and Emma.

Bottom right, left to right: Katy, Louise, Dad, me, Mum, Toni and Emma.

Top left: My beautiful wife Sheena.

Top right: Four of my little girls – Toni, Louise, Emma and Katy.

Middle: With Sheena and our youngest little girl Nikki. On the left is my brother-in-law Mark Wheeler.

Bottom: The family together. (*Clockwise from left*) Katy, Toni, me, Sheena, Emma, Louise, Nikki.

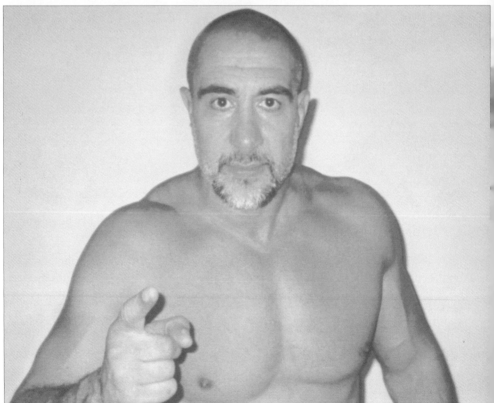

Top: When Kate Kray suggested that my nose was a bit bigger than it might be, there was only one option – a nose job. But it didn't stop me working the door…

Bottom: You ain't coming in!

get another one. Come on, mate, it's fucking best in the long run.'

'No way, we carry on.'

He wouldn't budge, and I could see this was shaping up to be a family fight unless something was done about it in bloody quick time. 'All right, Mark, I'll take the dog home. My garden's bigger than yours and I've got a shed I can keep him in. I'll get the fuckin' dog better on me own if that's the way it has to be.'

So I get Capital Cinema home and take it for a walk round the garden, round the park, bring him home. Sheena takes him out for a walk, gives him a lot of exercise, gets him fit quick. Me brother-in-law comes round at night, takes it out for walks, round and round. But it's still limping.

For breakfast, the dog has two eggs, a bowl of cornflakes with a pint of milk, and best mincemeat. This goes on for ages.

Six weeks later, the dog is still limping, so I took him back to see the bloody trainer.

'John, what the fuck's wrong with this dog? It's still limping.'

'Shouldn't be. What you doin', takin' it out for walks regular?'

'Yeah.'

'Giving it the right diet.'

'Yeah, 'course I am.'

'Well, give it another couple of weeks.'

But it wasn't gonna get another couple of weeks. Four days after I'd been to see John, my second daughter Toni, who was just four years old by then, was playing with the greyhound in the back garden. She was runnin' after it like little kids do when suddenly Capital Cinema turned round fast.

Sheena heard the screams from the kitchen. She came runnin'.

The dog had jumped up and bit Toni on the ear; blood was flowing. My little baby was crying. I came belting down the garden, tryin' to calm things down, but the bloody dog had taken a big bite out of Toni's ear. I knew we'd have to take her up the hospital as quickly as possible and I thought, Bloody National Health Service. She was a brave little girl, but Toni still has part of her right earlobe missing; they wouldn't graft anything back on for her.

So, the fuckin' dog had to go. We couldn't have it at the house any more. It was never intended to be a pet, it was a machine and now it had just bitten one of me daughters.

John said, 'OK, bring the dog back. I'll get it fit, you've put in enough time and effort.'

So me and the brother-in-law took it back to the trainer. He looked at it, touched it, murmured that it looked all right, but when he walked it, the dog was still limping.

'How many times a day you been walkin' it?' he asked me.

'About five times a day.'

'How many miles?'

'About a mile each time.'

'Well, he should be really fit, the time you've had him.'

Then John turned the dog's paws upside-down, and goes, 'Look, the fuckin' paws are down to the skin, they're bleedin! Have you been walking this dog on a pavement?'

'Erm, yes, John,' I said sheepishly.

'Well, you've worn its fucking pads out, that's why the dog's limping. This dog was fit months back. You are meant to walk these dogs on sand or on grass, not on the bloody road!

'No wonder the dog had a go at Toni. It was hurt, it was in pain, it was angry ...'

So John kept the dog for another couple of weeks; then we got it back on the track and it suddenly won for us at 10-1. But he was never the same dog after that first period of lameness.

But then one day it couldn't do it no more. It died on the track. Sad, that was. It was taking up the race on the rails again and, fuck me, if it didn't hit another bastard pot-hole in the sand. It collapsed, broke its leg, and the vet put it down. Bit of a sad ending there to old Capital Cinema. Mark was gutted as usual, lots of tears, and he wrote a glowing tribute to the dog which was published in the *Sporting Life*. Even the fucking kennel staff put on a memorial race and presented me and Mark with a porcelain model of the dog.

Mark loved the dog so much he even went on to christen his son Benjamin – after Big Bad Ben.

I went and bought another dog called Clog Arsed Grand and it won one in four races.

* * *

But my gambling in those days wasn't just confined to the dog track. If there was any money left, not needed for the home, I'd have a bet. Cards, dogs and the horses were me favourites, but I'd often go down Stanley's Casino in Margate and have a roll. I loved it there, 'cos even if you never won, they'd always give you steak and chips – so you got summat to eat.

And a fella named Theo Michaels, used to run this trendy wine bar underneath the casino. He was havin' trouble with the local authority licensing at the time and he would keep a book and write your name in it, plus the fact you were gonna eat. Then he could serve you drinks at the bar. But this one night, I was down there with my mate, Greek Tony, and another pal called Mick Peters who was a Gumbarro, one of the best men at my wedding, and we didn't wanna eat but wanted a drink. He said there was a bit of a problem that night and we couldn't drink. So we decided to leave, but just as we were goin', he served some other people, quite a few of 'em.

'Oi,' I said. 'How comes they can get a drink and we can't?'

'I wouldn't serve you even if you were my own brother,' shouted Michaels, really angry, for no apparent reason. It was embarrassin'.

It was particularly embarrassing because Mick Peters was my Gumbarro. He had signed the ribbon at my wedding and paid money for the privilege of being my Gumbarro for life. You must never upset your Gumbarro, and whatever he says is right. You must never argue with him or shout at him or be disrespectful to him. You are closer than friends, closer than mates. So to be disrespected in front of Mick was very bad indeed.

So I said to Michaels, 'Right, we'll come back another time when you've calmed down, mate.' But when he shouted again, I thought, I'm not having this. So I told him to fuck it, if he wanted to shout at me, I could shout louder. Then we decided to leave, walked out and went up to the casino.

Then this Michaels bloke came running out of the wine bar and he was shouting again, 'Who are you givin' it the big 'un in my bar in front of all my staff?'

So I looked at him and thought, What the fuck are you on about? He had embarrassed me. So I stepped down two steps and went *bang*! – I hit him, but he dodged it. That's when my mate whispered to me that he was the British and European Tae Kwon Do champion. I threw another left, and he dodged that. We were standing close together and all of a sudden he aimed a kick to the side of me head. So I put me hand up and blocked it. The pain made me scream out. He had caught my finger and broken it. So this time I caught him with a left in the eye and he staggered back.

I said, 'Have you had enough, you cunt?'

'Yeah.'

'Well, count yourself lucky or I'll give you some more.'

What he didn't realise was that my little finger was throbbing and all I wanted to do was go home. And what he also didn't realise was that, behind him, was all his kitchen staff waving these bloody big knives. That's when I knew it was time to go.

But he did me a bit of a favour, 'cos at the casino my finger was hurtin' so bad I couldn't put the chips on. So I decided to jack it in and for once I went home with some money in me pocket.

The trouble with casino gambling, though, is you're never in charge. There's always someone else dealing and I don't like that. I like to deal meself 'cos that's the only way I can be sure I'm dealing the right cards. If you want to deal yourself an ace, for instance, it's simplicity itself. First shuffle the cards until you've got the ace firmly on the bottom of the pack and, as you go round in the deal, suddenly look up to the door or window or something. You can bet everybody in the card school will look up too, and that's when you palm the ace from the bottom. It's fuckin' simple. It's always worth doing in three-card brag because if you ended up with an ace that was a very high card to be holding. And then you'd just go fuckin' blind on it. Another way of palming the ace is to start talking as you're dealing because then the rest of the players in the card school will look at your face rather than the cards you're dealing. Keep eye contact with 'em and they won't notice a bloody thing.

I enjoyed gambling during that period after Peter had tried to turn over the firm. It might seem fuckin' strange but it gave me an ability to focus, and I'd gamble any time of the day or night. I've won money and I've lost money but, in the end, you usually end up losing. It's not really about the money, it's about the thrill of it all.

I remember one year, though, when I was pretty young, Sheena and I were going on holiday to Cyprus and she says to me, 'Stellakis, pop down the bank and get the holiday money, will you?'

'Sure, darling, won't be long.'

So I picked up £500 from the bank and, on me way back, I thought, A little bet and we could have a really brilliant holiday, so I went into the nearest bookies.

I had a bet on a couple of horses and my luck was in; it seemed like money for old rope. So I put some more on and won again. Then my luck turned and I started losing, but I didn't think fuck all about it, I was still up on the £500. But instead of walking away, I put half of it on one bloody horse which was a right fucking nag and lost. Then shit or bust I had to put the rest on the last race to try and get the holiday money back. Yeah, that's right, it came up bust. I felt miserable, but it wasn't 'cos I'd lost the money, after all, I had had the thrill of the race. Nah, I felt bad 'cos Sheena would go fuckin' mad when she found out, and she did. She called me everythin' under the sun. I was a worthless, useless husband. It went on for ages. In the end, she made me go and see me dad and borrow the holiday money from him.

He disliked anything to do with gambling and, when he heard the story, the first thing he did was phone up Gamblers Anonymous.

'Hey, Dad,' I said. 'You're over-reacting, ain't ya?'

'No, son, you've got to be straightened out and these people are the ones to do it.'

They advised Dad not to give me any money under any circumstances and that I should go to one of their meetings.

'Well, if that's what you think's right, Dad,' I said. 'But I've learned my lesson. And I don't see why Sheena should go without a fucking holiday 'cos of what I done.'

I kept this up for a bit and then said, 'Go on, Dad, lend us a bob or two. If not for me then for Sheena to have a decent time. She can go to Cyprus on her own; it'll do her the world of good.'

Of course, I knew Dad would never let Sheena go on holiday without me. And so, eventually, he caved in and lent us the money. As he was handing it over I thought, Have I got time to get down to that fuckin' betting shop before the plane takes off? But then I thought, Stilks, not this time, mate, not this time.

The trouble with gambling is you do sometimes do down the people you don't want to fuckin' hurt in the first place. Take my mate Mick Lavell, or 'Scotty' as he was known. He's a bit of a gambler as well, a bit of a hard nut from Greenock in Scotland. He came down to South London 'cos he was a right hard bastard, had been in a gang, and the police were after him.

We met through another friend of mine, Pierre La Riviere. So I open up the paper one day and I see this horse I fancy, but I hadn't got no money. What the fuck do I do? I know, I'll get in touch with Mick.

Now, he was working as the manager of a sweet shop in Abbey Wood, so I went down there and told him that I fancied this horse. 'But I ain't got no money,' I said.

'I ain't got none either.'

'You have.'

'I ain't. Where?'

'You're the manager of this sweet shop, ain't ya? Well, you've got the money in the till.'

'Nah, Stilks, nah,' he said. 'I can't do that.' And in the next breath, 'Are you sure this horse is gonna win?'

'Yeah, course it is, it's favourite, can't fucking lose. Richard Dunwoody's on it.'

So I convinced him. There was £200 in the till so I said, 'That'll do, we'll have that on it.'

I bombed round the betting office and bang, put it on. And it lost. Back to the sweet shop. 'Mick, it lost.'

'Fuck, what am I gonna do?'

'Well, how much more have you taken while I was away?' I say.

'About another 80 quid.'

'Gimme that and we'll have to put it on a fucking 4-1 shot to get the money back plus a bit of profit.'

'All right. Who's gonna pick the horse?'

'I will,' I say. 'I can't lose two in a row.'

I put it on. It's going well, jumping the last, and then *bang!* it's fallen over.

'Mick, it lost.'

Mick's holding his head and squeezing it. 'What we gonna

do?' he's moaning. 'Stilks, you just go. Get fucking out of here now. I'll try and sort it out. Leave it with me.'

I thought he might spin his guv'nor a line or summat and get out of it that way, so a couple of days later I phone up the sweet shop only to be told that Mick's no longer there and that he has gone to Scotland. I eventually got in touch with him and asked what had happened.

He said, 'Well, after you left I took all the rest of the money in the till, took all the cigarettes and cigars, put them all in a suitcase and left for Scotland.'

After he had sold the cigarettes and spent all the money, he came back down to London and got a job as the manager of a video shop in Woolwich.

He was only there one week when I walked in.

As soon as he sees me, Mick starts shouting, 'No … no … no … whatever it is, the answer is fucking no.'

But I'm very persuasive – and we've done it again.

This time, Mick was staying round his mum's house in Abbey Wood and that's where the Old Bill went round and got him. What he didn't know was that they were looking for him for robbing the first shop, too. He took the rap for both of those jobs and ended up doing 18 months inside. And he never said a word about me. That's the kind of fucking bloke he was. He even used to write to me from prison.

When he came out, we went for a game of pool in the Fox under the Hill and there was a look of unfinished business in Mick's eyes. I knew something was gonna trigger him off.

He goes, 'Stilks, you're givin' it the big 'un to everyone round here, but I heard you weren't so fucking hard when you were younger. Bit of a wimp I've heard 'em say.'

'Mick, we're good friends, but if you're offering me out, let's go over the park.'

Now, Mick's family were boxers. His brother Gerry Lavell fought for England about ten times. So we shaped up and I hit him as hard as I could on the arm. Me hand's gone fucking numb, I can't feel nothin' but I'm still pretending I'm all right. Mick has thrown a few punches, but I've managed to get him round and I've got him in an arm-lock. But then I'm over and I've twisted me knee. But I've still got the arm-lock on and trying to keep it on him as hard as possible. He was a big lad and I knew that if I gave him even the slightest chance he'd do me. But Mick was obviously in a bit of pain from the arm and says, 'Stilks, I was only joking.' So we managed to stop fighting and as we were good friends I decided to carry him home holding his arm and he took the weight off me leg.

We looked a right sight coming off that park. But deep down we were friends, and we have remained friends ever since.

I think Mick must have brooded on the time he spent in prison for those shop robberies and, after a few drinks, he had to get it out of his fucking system. I don't blame him at all for that. I s'pose I would have done the same.

The fight with Mick, short and sweet though it was, had taught me something. Nah, it wasn't getting your mates to take the blame, fuck that. It was that I liked the rough and tumble of getting in there, getting up close, getting in the middle of it. I liked fighting for my life, as I'd always fought.

But now I was off the bleedin' door game I decided to pick myself up and open another gym. PecS, the one I had with Peter Hayford, was a sad memory, and that's all it was now, a memory. So I started scouting around for a place and found a site right near the Station Hotel, on top of an Iceland store. It was bigger than PecS, and things had moved on a lot since then. Now instead of just weights there were all sorts of Nautilus machines and things like that the punters were demanding that would do everything from lat pull-downs to calf stretches and abdominal crunches.

I sorted out the lease on the place, got the financing for a few machines, and I was up and runnin' in no time.

Fitness was the big new craze towards the end of the Eighties and I thought, Right, I'm fuckin' well in here. This could turn into a right little money-spinner. And this time I'm gonna do it meself.

And I honestly meant it. I knuckled down and got the gym, Bodywise, off the ground.

At the time, I was living in Bexleyheath in a four-bedroom house in Oldfield Road. We'd been there a few years and the family was quite settled. It looked like that was where we were going to stay. One night, me and the wife jumped into bed like normal and, being a heavy sleeper, I put me head down and I was out like a light in 30 seconds. Next thing I feel is Sheena nudging me in the ribs with her elbow.

'Whassup, love?' I said.

'I can hear something.'

'Yeah? Go back to sleep.' And I turned over.

'But I can hear something downstairs, Stellarg,' said Sheena – Stellarg was what she'd started calling me.

'OK then,' I said. 'Go downstairs, and if there's someone there, come back up and get me. Goodnight.'

But that's when I heard something. I jumped out of bed naked and ran downstairs just in time to see this fella drop me video recorder and run out the back door. With that, I chased him through the patio doors. He bolted up the road and I followed him. But being naked, and with all them little fucking stones on the road, I never got far.

Unknown to me, Sheena had phoned 999. So they came hurtling round the corner and there I was in the middle of the road … naked. The neighbours were peering out of their windows at all the commotion so I dived back into the house to get a towel.

The Old Bill followed me. 'What have they taken?' said one 'em.

'How do I know? I'm only just up.'

So I turned to the wife. 'You talk to 'em, love. It's four in the morning. I'm going back to bed. I ain't finished sleeping.'

With that, I jumped back into bed and I was out cold again. But after that incident, Sheena had a lot of trouble sleeping. The burglary had been an invasion of her privacy. I knew it wouldn't be very long before she would want to move house, and I didn't blame her. That Bexleyheath was bloody full of villains!

Mind you, when I put the insurance claim in and put down what was missing, the insurance company wrote back and said that I had undervalued the property that was nicked and gave me nearly twice as much as I asked for. So that was a result. And if anyone's reading this who know's the cunt that burgled my house, will you thank them for me?

One weekend, while we were still in the Oldfield Road house, I was home with Sheena when there was a knock on the door. I opened it and recognised this fella's face but I didn't really know him. It turned out to be a bloke called Chris Olley.

'Wass happenin'? Come in.'

'They're opening this massive nightclub, the biggest nightclub in the South-East. It's going to be called Stars and we want you to work there.'

'Nah, I've had enough mate. I'm gonna stay in with the wife. Ain't that right, Sheena?'

'That's what you said Stellarg,' she replied.

But Olley wasn't really listening. He said there would be about 16 doormen and that he was the head one, but because I was well known they wanted me in the team as well.

He was givin' me all this fuckin' flannel. 'You're the one, Stilks. You're a bloody legend in this game and the owner only wants the best people on the door. This ain't no ordinary nightclub, Stilks, this is gonna be the classiest joint ever seen. It's gonna be as cool as London's West End clubs but it's gonna be miles bigger, better and louder. And I've been sent here to get you because everybody wants Stilks in at the beginning.'

'Cut the bollocks,' I said. 'How much?'

When he told me I thought, Wow, that's good, and then quite rightly asked for more.

'Whaddya think, Sheena, shall I go and have a look at it?'

'Why ask me? You will anyway.'

And so I did. Me and Chris went down there to eye it up before it opened. And he was right. This was a big fucking place. It was either gonna be a tremendous success or … I didn't even like to think what would happen if things started to get out of hand. I shuddered at the thought.

Stars was in a perfect place situated between New Cross, Lewisham, Woolwich and Thamesmead, through the tunnel from Bermondsey. All the mugs and all the thugs from all over the area would come.

'OK, Chris,' I said. 'I'll think about it.'

'Right, then why don't you start a week on Friday like the rest of us? Big opening party, Stilks, you'll love it, mate.'

7

STAR STRUCK

**WHENEVER YOU'RE IN TROUBLE,
SWAP JACKETS.**
STILKS

I WASN'T READY FOR STARS. IT WAS A HELLUVA PLACE. IT HELD ABOUT 2,000 RAVERS AND HAD BEEN RENOVATED BY A GUY NAMED MICHAEL ROSS WHO DID ALL THE WORK HIMSELF WITH THE MANAGER NAMED KEITH BROWN. IT WAS ON THREE FLOORS, AN OLD SORT OF PICTURE HOUSE-TYPE PLACE WITH A MASSIVE RECEPTION, PLENTY OF BARS, A HUGE DANCE FLOOR, AND DJS THAT PLAYED ALL THE LATEST HOUSE MUSIC AND GARAGE. IT WAS AN ABSOLUTE WINNER; IT COULDN'T FAIL.

I said to Chris Olley that if I was gonna come along, I'd have to take two men with me that I could trust 100 per cent, that would be behind me no matter what and who I could trust with my life. One was Dave Killroy, who I gave a job to when he was 16 and worked with me for ten years; the other close friend was Dave Bowdery, who had also worked with me for a decade. Bowdery has the most dangerous right hand I've ever seen in my life.

'You can have 'em,' says Olley. Will you join the team?'

'Awright.'

First night I was there, I recognised a few of the faces. There were some doormen that had been around other clubs, and one or two that had worked for me before Peter turned the firm over; others I'd had some confrontation with. I gave those bastards a knowing wink. I wasn't head doorman here, Chris Olley was, I was just another of the blokes. But it wasn't gonna take me long ... so I checked the place out. Yeah, yeah, I was thinking. Nice place, nice and new, good facilities, easy for handling the crowds and getting' 'em out if anything kicks off. Then I had a look round, checking for access and all that stuff and that's when I saw it ... I couldn't believe my fuckin' eyes. Right next door to the club was a bloody great hospital! I thought, Yes, just what we might need. Fantastic. For once, the Bloody National Health Service looked like it was coming up trumps. If this club was any good, we could keep that place next door going for years.

We were told by the owners that we had to take it easy. We were being watched by the Old Bill, and it was a new club. Michael Ross had put a lot of money into it, and was paying us well. He didn't want it shut down until he'd got his money back at least!

Stars was perfectly situated in Greenwich for all the mugs and thugs from East London and the South-East. All the gangs and all the local idiots from all around would eventually find their way to the place because it had late drinking and it was a new club. At the beginning, there were always large queues and you'd get the girls and regular punters in quite early. We were fucking choosy about who we'd let in in them days. But as time went on, it became less busy and we'd let in anybody. That's when the problems started …

When a club's successful and doing well, you can choose your customers and kick the riff-raff out. You can make up any dress code and rules, like the usual 'no jeans and trainers', or even 'hey, mate, your hair ain't combed the right way, fucking hop it.' The trouble really starts when the club's on the slide.

The fights at Stars didn't begin for a few months after it opened and then they were your usual fights that you'd have in any pub or club where drinks have been spilled or someone's chatting up another bloke's girl. It got worse when the drug-dealers and the gangs turned up. The gangs would stand in different corners of the club jeering at each other, and that's when the aggro really would start. We'd try to keep most of the dealers out, but some would get through or new ones turn up. It was mainly Ecstasy or cocaine, and if a dealer got to know that any of the doormen liked drugs, then he'd slip them some to get in. I wouldn't work with any doormen who sold drugs, and made sure they were sacked if I saw any of that stuff goin' on. But if they wanted to use it themselves that was up to them.

I remember an Italian guy who used to hang out with the *EastEnders* stars. He used to give a wrap of coke to one of the doormen every time he came in. Many of the *EastEnders* stars used to come along. There was that ginger nut, Patsy summat, and the one with that Wellhard dog, lots of 'em. There was Camilla Parker Bowles' son there, too. There were all kinds of idiots, everyone popped in, plenty of stars there.

Once when it kicked off in there, it frightened the shit out of me. It was 2.00am, home time, and we were asking people to go. 'Make a move now please, that's right, that way, sir. Keep moving ...' There were two gentlemen in Crombies, looking like local gangsters, not normal punters. Everyone else was movin', but they were standin' there drinking their fuckin' beer. They were the last ones left in the club and still refused to move.

One of the other doormen, a gorilla of a bloke, came over and asked them to drink up quickly as it was way past time. And then as one of the Crombie-clad fellas lifted his glass to his mouth, the doorman pushed the glass straight into his face. *Crunch*! The bloke went down. His mate, who was shocked, tried to move when the doorman hit him and he was out cold on the floor. I thought, Fuckin' hell, this is a bit over the top for just a couple of late drinkers!

The first bloke's face was bleedin' from the ears where the glass had cut him up and he was out on the floor with his eyes open, just staring up at the ceiling. Then the doorman walked over to one of his mates watching and whispered, 'I love a good curry', ran back to the guy on the floor, jumped up in the air, and landed right on his victim's head. I thought, Oh for fuck's sake!

I'll always remember the sound, this hollow ringing thud that went all round this huge empty club. That sound will stay with me for ever.

I looked down at the bloke on the floor and my stomach started to knot as if I was about to gag. Blood was squirting out of his ears; it was spraying along the floor and up at the bar. Blood fucking everywhere. It seemed obvious to me that the bloke must be dead. All the flesh under his right eye socket was peeled back and ripped off where he had taken the force of the boot smashing into his face.

His mate who had been out cold had woken up, taken one look at the fucking scene, and bolted for the door. He was gone. I went over to the opposite side of the club and told the manager, 'I'm going home, I wasn't even here tonight. There's a bloke over there; if he's dead, I wasn't here. He ain't moving.'

There was congealed blood all over the floor and across the bar.

The guv'nor goes, 'Mop down the bar, wash the floor, get rid of as much blood as you can.'

'What about the body?'

'Dunno, Stilks, you figure something out.'

So I grab one of the other doormen, most of whom were just fuckin' standin' around looking shocked. 'Come on, we've got to move the body out of the club. Anywhere but here. Now give me a fucking hand.'

And just as we were about to haul him up off the floor, there was a slight stirring, a slight movement. I thought, Thank God for that.

'Here,' I said to the other doorman. 'Help me drag him into the kitchen.' His Crombie was well fucked by now. But we managed to clean him up a bit although it was still a horrible sight, his face mangled and smashed and hair matted with blood. But he was starting to come round and we managed to sit him on a stool.

'Come on, mate, we'll just clean you up a bit and get you to hospital. Come on, mate, you can make it,' I was saying. He was a big fucking lump and that's about the only thing that was going to save him.

With that, he reaches up and grabs one of the kitchen knives, one with a good 8in blade and tries to stumble out of the door back into the bar. There's still blood trickling out of his ears and he's muttering about '… havin' to kill 'im … havin' to kill 'im …' I thought, Fuck me, this is turning into a nightmare. If he makes it into the bar it'll be the doorman who'll kill *him*.

So I dash between him and the door, 'You ain't going fuckin' nowhere, mate. Before I let you go out there, you're gonna have to fight me with that knife.' He goes to push me out of the way and I grab his hand, quickly put it into a wristlock, and disarm him in seconds. He could barely stand up so unless he had made a lucky lunge at me and connected, I didn't feel I was under any threat. I threw the knife on the floor, quickly kicked it into a far corner of the kitchen and then called one of the other guys to help me get him to hospital.

'If he can walk a bit, I'll help ya, Stilks, we can get him next door easy,' he said.

'Don't be such a fucking pillock,' I said. 'If he goes next door, you might as well say goodbye to your job and this club, they'll close it down. That hospital's all right for scrapes and bruises, but this bloke's been fuckin' steam-rollered mate. Throw him in a cab. He'll get to a hospital on his own. And don't worry about the Old Bill. See what he's wearing? A fucking Crombie. He ain't gonna do no squealin'.'

But it was a terrifying night. If someone pulls out a gun and shoots, then it's over and done. But this was horrifying. Imagine a balloon full of water and then you burst it. That was just like this bloke's fuckin' head, blood spraying out of his ears, down his nose, through his mouth, gushing it was. At one stage, I thought we all might be on a murder charge. We were gonna drag the body into the car park and say we'd seen nothin'.

We never saw the guy again, he never came back to Stars – probably the brain damage.

That happened about six months after Stars opened and, as time went on, the reputation of the place grew. The music was hardcore house and garage and the drug scene surrounding it started growing with it. The punters who came to the club were either E'd out of their heads or they'd be sniffing in the toilets. In fact, the toilets got so bad at one time that they were out-of-bounds to all the doormen except me and my mate Dave Bowdery. The rest of the muscle were too frightened to go in there. Normal customers, if they went to the Gents toilets, would be robbed. It was a frightening place.

There were about six or seven cubicles and they were opposite the normal unrinals. One day there was a bloke bleeding in there and the manager, bald-headed Keith Brown, ordered me and Dave to go down and see what was goin' on.

We went down there and there was this half-caste geezer layin' on the floor in a pool of blood with blood spurting out of his neck. It looked a recent stabbing. But it wasn't that shocking to me and Dave 'cos things had got so bad, and the police had been in the club so many times, it was almost on the verge of shutting down. The licence had been taken away for 18-year-olds and now you had to be 21 to get in. But that didn't make much difference.

I said to Keith Brown, 'Right, Keith, it looks like another stabbing, shall I phone for an ambulance?'

'No, we don't want to bring any more attention to ourselves. Just pick him up and put him outside by the bins.'

'You're having a fuckin' laugh, ain't ya, this guy's seriously hurt.'

'Just put him outside,' said Brown. 'And you've got 15 minutes to clean up the toilet so it can be used again.'

The place was getting like that. A stabbing didn't mean much as long as it was hushed up. And all the time there was a bloody hospital next door. But it was starting to get to everyone who was working the security. You had to be constantly alert and on your toes 'cos there could be trouble lurking anywhere. There wasn't one night when there wasn't an incident. Even I was starting to flag under the pressure and the stress. I started feeling tired all the time, even when I first got to work, let alone at the end of a night when it might go off two or three times.

That's when one of the other doormen said, 'Here, Stilks, have a sniff of this, it keeps you up.'

'Whaddya mean "keeps you up"? Let's have a try.'

So I sniffed this white powder up me nose and said, 'Well, that ain't done fuck all for me, that ain't done nothin'.'

But I'd taken it at 9.00pm and I still wasn't tired at 3.00am. I went home and even started phoning people up and chatting to them 'cos I wasn't tired.

The following week, back at work some of the others were sniffin' outta their heads and asked me if I wanted a line. 'Nah, I've told ya, it does fuck all for me.'

'What do you mean, it woke you up last week and kept you awake, didn't it?'

''Course it didn't. I just livened up that's all. That stuff did fuck all I tell ya.'

'Then what was you doin' phonin' us all up for a chat in the middle of the night?' one of 'em said.

And I thought, Maybe he's got a point, maybe it did do something. So I said, 'OK, give me another fucking line of that shit.' So I had another little sniff but I was still convinced it was doing fuck all to me.

'Then do a fucking bigger line,' said one of the doormen who could hardly stop talking.

I said, 'Right. If you come and do what I like doing, I'll do a big one.'

'What do you like doing, Stilks?'

'I like going down the dogs and doing me money.'

'Right, we'll go down there tomorrow, do the money, and then you keep your half of the bargain.'

And that's how I came to snort my first really big line of coke. It got me livened up, got me goin'. For the first time, I found meself tapping me fingers and that's really unusual because I don't dance and won't dance, except for that time on my wedding day. Dancing is for girls, not for hard bastards. But here I was tapping me fingers to the fucking music. Something was definitely happening.

It started with one line a night, then a couple of sniffs, then three a night and, as the weeks went by, we were doing more and more of the stuff. Then someone got the bright idea that we should carry on snorting coke after the club had closed.

So we'd all end up back at Bodywise, my gym. We'd be talking all night long, most of it I suppose now was a load of shit, but that's what it's like when you're outta your head on coke. You'll talk about anything, sound knowledgeable, think you're being witty, and if everyone else is coked up, too, it don't matter 'cos they're talking an equal amount of drivel and shit. This would go on until about five or six o'clock in the morning. Then all the wives would start phonin' up giving their blokes a right bollockin' until they went home. Most of the blokes on the door at Stars were now going to the gym after the club had closed and tooting up. The coke was getting out of hand but nobody gave a shit. Most of it was being given to us anyway. I never sold any and I never had to pay for any, it was fucking perfect. And it went on like that for a couple of months until I wasn't getting it free any more and I thought it was rude of me to go and ask the other doormen for some of theirs. They'd been giving it to me 'cos they thought it was a right joke to get Stilks wound up and coked out. But now the joke had worn off and it was costing them money.

OK, I thought, I'll have to go and buy some.

That's when one of the blokes told me it was £50 for a gram.

'Fuck off,' I said. 'I ain't paying 50 quid for it.'

But what was I gonna do? And that's when I twigged it.

I turned to my mate Dave and said, 'Dave, Dave, see that cunt over there, that's the fourth time he's been to the toilet in the last hour.'

'Yeah.'

'Well, we're doormen, ain't we?'

'Yeah.'

'Well, next time he goes down there we'll follow, wait 'til he gets into the toilet and look over the partition. And I'll bet you he's having a sniff. Then we're gonna search him, take his sniff off him, and then we've got his coke and we ain't paid for it.'

So down we go, waiting outside, and we nab him.

'You've been sniffin', ain't ya, mate?' I say.

'No.'

'Well, we're gonna search you anyway.'

And, sure enough, he had a wrap of coke on him, which we immediately seized. I then gave him two choices. We could either phone the Old Bill and tell 'em, in which case they'd come and bust him and take his drugs, or we could take his drugs and let him go. Being a sensible fucking chap, he went for the second choice and me and Dave were on our way. Instead of looking down at the dance floor to see who was causing trouble and fights, we then became more interested in watching the Gents toilets and spotting the coke sniffers going back and forth.

We didn't have to worry about paying for drugs any more. The place was packed with coke heads. There must have been half the bleedin' Columbian economy going back and forth to those toilets.

It worked like a dream. We'd look over the partition from the next cubicle, spot the coke sniffer, then bang on the door and give him our ultimatum. And would you believe it – not one of the fuckers ever wanted us to call the police. Funny that, they'd just hand over the sniffs and be on their way.

Anyway, one night we went down to search the toilets and heard this big snorting noise coming from one of the cubicles. Me and Dave looked at each other and started rubbing our hands. Yes, here was another one, I thought.

So we knocked on the door. 'Out ya come, mate,' I said. 'We know you're in there having a sniff. Come out and hand it over or we'll come in and throw you fucking well out. Come on, out ya come.' We're banging on the door. The door slowly opens and the biggest black guy I've ever seen is standing there with a huge knife in his hand. He must have been about 6ft 3in and powerfully built.

I swallowed deeply and looked at Dave. He looked at me. We both looked at the geezer in the bog and not one word was said between us. But we were the doormen, the tough guys, and so we had to carry on. If we showed that we were losing our bottle, he was either gonna stab us or think we were mugs and just walk away. So I read him the usual rights.

'We heard you sniffin', mate, so you've got two choices. Either you share it with us or we call the police and you share it with them.'

The black guy didn't say a word. He just stared at us, holding this huge knife in his right hand. Sweat was starting to break out under my collar. I daren't take my eyes off the knife just in case he was going to make a lunge.

Then he slightly waved the blade, indicating that me and Dave should go in the cubicle. Well, you can imagine the scene. Here's this huge geezer, a good 20st, and me and Dave, who were hardly undernourished, trying to cram into this fucking toilet.

Anyway, the black guy dips the end of the knife into his wrap of cocaine, all the time holding us both with his staring eyes, and he slowly lifts the point of the knife up to my nose.

'Nah,' I go. 'My mate first.' I wanted to see what the geezer was gonna do. I wasn't having him fucking slicing me. Dave looks at me as if to say, 'Thank you, you cunt,' and then snorts the coke off the end of the knife blade. Everybody relaxes a bit and even the black guy had a little smile.

So we back out of the door and I shout so that everyone can hear, 'And don't let us catch you again. If we do, you won't get off so fucking lightly. It'll be the Old Bill, mate. You've been bloody well warned. Off you go.'

And as he slowly walks out of the Gents, me and Dave look at each other as if to say, 'That was bloody close.'

So I say to Dave, 'How many times have I fucking well told you? Look over the partition first! Got that?'

We'd been working at Stars quite a while by then. There was a big new doorman called John, a giant of a man, 6ft 7in. He had huge, long hands. I saw him have a fight once with someone I thought was quite tasty with his fists. But this bloke John had such a long reach he just went *bang*! *bang*! *bang*! and knocked him out. But it doesn't matter how big you are when you're in a major club like Stars, you have to work in twos.

One night, we were asking people to leave when all of a sudden someone shouts out, 'John's been done, John's been done.'

'What the fuck's been happenin'?' I said.

'The gang from Thamesmead, they've done him,' says this other doorman.

The gang from Thamesmead! I thought. They're fuckin' 18-year-olds. John's a giant.

Well, what happened was, he asked one of them to leave and while he was doing so, another one of the gang jumped off the balcony on to his back. They've all rushed him together and brought him down, and kicked the shit out of him.

Fortunately, this time John was taken to the hospital next door. John had been working the doors for about 15 years and he was one of the most professional fucking blokes I had ever worked with. But that night was his last night and he was never able to work again because of what the Thamesmead gang had done. That's how rough this club was getting.

A week later, it's all kicking off again and all the doormen scramble inside to see these eight geezers walking round the club shoutin', 'We're the firm … we're the firm.' I recognised some of them from the Thamesmead mob who had done John the week before, plus some other faces.

So I called the doormen over and told them all to keep together. We'd rush the gang of blokes and fucking well take them out. Normally when you rush 'em, you take 'em out one at a time. But this bleedin' mob wanted to stand and fight us. OK then, I thought, here we go.

We were havin' a good fight with them when one of them pulls out this knuckle-duster and goes *bang*! to one of our men. The fight had taken about 20 seconds and then we stepped back to see what the injuries were. One of the doormen had a bad cut over his eye from the duster and the yobs were all backed-up into a corner. But they were still shoutin', 'We're the firm … we're the firm.'

There was blood on their faces, torn jackets, shirts. We looked the same, but I was thinking, How the fuck are we going to get them out? I was looking to see who the ringleader was and recognised the bloke who had jumped off the balcony and attacked John. I thought, Right, he'll fucking do. If we drag him out it'll break up the strength of the others. So me and Dave grab him, stick him in a head-lock and haul him away through the club letting him have it, while the rest of the scum were chucked out the back door.

We were dragging the ringleader through the dance floor, up the stairs, along past the bar and out to the corridor at the front. All the time he was squealing while we put more pressure on the head-lock. 'Shut up,' shouted Dave, who then smashed one into his face. 'That's for John.' He was still struggling and Dave can hit, so he was letting him have it. We got him into the corner and was just about to make sure he went down, when I heard this strange hollering and whooping sound.

I turned round and thought, Fuck me, the whole club has turned against us. From the balcony and all around, they were throwing glasses and beer bottles which started raining down on us. We were trying to sort out a problem and there was fucking glass showering down. 'Get him out, GET HIM OUT,' I shouted at Dave. We were trying to protect ourselves from the glass with arms up while keeping the cunt in a head-lock and somehow edging towards the front door.

We managed to get there, get outside and close the door behind us as bottles whizzed past and then smashed into the door.

The rest of the so-called 'firm' had been frog-marched out of the back door. So now all the doormen were outside and a riot was going on in the club. That's when I heard the sirens in the distance. The Old Bill were on their way. The manager must have phoned the police when he saw things getting out of hand and their arrival was spectacular.

The road was immediately cordoned off and then the police approached the club with battering rams and horses. I'd been petrol bombed by the bastards at the Camden, had bricks thrown at me at the Plough and the Station and had too many knives pulled on me to bother talking about. But this was the first time I'd been caught up in a full-scale cavalry charge.

The doors to the club went flying open as the police stormed the place and we brought up the rear. Inside, it was mayhem. Glass was everywhere and the thugs were going wild. The police waded in and I saw three of 'em beating the shit out of one young bloke. They were covered in body armour and started throwing everyone out of the club and into this line of wagons they'd brought with them.

I was well psyched up by now and wanted to hit someone badly. Not only had us doormen somehow lost control of the situation, but the Ol' Bill had been called in, and that was fucking humiliation.

'Hands off, mate,' I said to one of the police. 'That bloke's a punter, he ain't no trouble-maker.'

'Yeah, well let him explain that one down the station. This place is getting out of control. I wouldn't like to think what your chances are of getting the licence renewed.'

And he was right, Stars looked like it was down on its knees. And the bloke that had started the latest trouble, the geezer from the 'firm' who had jumped John, was pleading fucking innocence. But later, he got done for shooting a doorman in another club and now he's doing life.

We all realised that unless we got a grip on the situation at the club, it would be closed down and we'd all lose our jobs. So we decided to pile on the muscle big time. Keep out anyone who even vaguely looked like they were out to cause trouble. One more incident like the riot and that would be it for Stars.

Yet less than a fortnight later, another fight broke out. I was up at the balcony looking down, and keepin' me eye on the Gents toilets. The other doormen rushed in and I didn't bother going down. It only looked like a little one and they could cope with it. But instead of coping with it, it started getting bigger and bigger and I thought, Fuckin' hell, and ran down there pushing all the people back.

I cleared the area and managed to get everyone standing in a big circle. The other doormen were chucking the yobbos out and I was there watching the doormen's backs. At the end, there was just me left there in the circle of about 400 people and slowly the circle started getting fuckin' smaller and smaller, and I was all alone.

'Aarghh, get back, get back,' I started shouting. Some of them retreated but others were getting braver when they realised I was all on my fuckin' own. They started taunting me – 'Think you're hard … think you're hard, do you?' and advancing towards me. That's when, out of the corner of me eye, I spotted one of the other doormen who had come back into the club. He smashed his way through the circle. 'Stay with me, Stilks, stay with me,' he shouted, grabbing my arm.

'Whatcha doin'?'

'Just stay with me, it'll be all right. Run for it when I say so.'

'OK.'

'Right, run now.'

And with that he sprayed this canister of CS gas into the circle while we shot out of the front door.

There was complete pandemonium in the club. The tear gas can be dangerous at close quarters and so everyone ran as fast as possible to the nearest exits. I'd never seen the club cleared so quickly, something like 2,000 people all out within bloody minutes.

Out in the street, I turned to the doorman who had saved me and said, 'Cheers, mate, where the fuck did you get that stuff?'

'Picked it up a couple of weeks ago. The Old Bill left it lying around after that near-riot we had. I thought, I bet that'll come in useful one day. What I didn't realise was that it would be so soon.'

He was right. Everything seemed to be spinning out of control. I was still sniffing coke but the thrill was going as I had to do more and more to stay alert and stay on top of things.

And I was getting in with the wrong crowd. There was one dealer I got to know, he's dead now, who asked me if I'd do him a few fuckin' favours, you know what I mean. If anyone owed him money or anything like that, he'd phone me up and say, 'Stilks, will you phone 'em and just give 'em a reminder.' And for that he'd give me a few hundred pounds worth.

I have strong morals and it took me to the age of 34 before I took any drugs, but I still wouldn't sell it or pass it on to anybody. But I was a grown man and if I had decided to take coke then that was it. I went from taking it once on a fucking Friday night to taking it on Friday and Saturday. Then I was working at another club on a Sunday so I'd take some more to get me through that night. And before I knew it, I started taking it on 'a long weekend', that was Thursday, Friday, Saturday and Sunday. Then the 'long weekend' ended up being the whole of the week and I was taking it every day. After a few weeks, I shook my head and thought, What the hell's happenin'? I've got to stop doin' this.

I was runnin' around like a maniac. There was meant to be a buzzer system at the club so that if anything went off, you could be at the exact spot in seconds. Stars was so big it was no use tryin' to find out where the trouble was, it took too long. But the buzzers didn't work and so someone had to come runnin' down to the fuckin' door to find anyone available to go and defuse the situation.

Runnin' from one end of the club to the other, I probably caused six fights meself, knocking people out of the way and spillin' drinks and that. And as I was running all over the place, I heard the head doorman Chris Olley shouting, 'Serve 'em up, Stilks, serve 'em up.'

Well, one night I really did have to serve someone up. I was standing on the door greeting the customers when this large guy comes in. He's got a bit of an accent, a scar on his face and some of his ear bitten off.

'Sorry, mate,' I say. 'You can't come in, no jeans.'

So he's standing around the front door being a bit of a nuisance.

'Out the way, mate, do us a favour, you're in the way of the customers. Can you let 'em through for us?' I said.

He's still standing there. 'How much a night do you get here?' he asks me. 'Where I come from, I probably get more than you do.'

'Listen, mate, I'm not interested in how much you get. Will you just fuckin' well stand aside.'

He doesn't budge and keeps goin' on, givin' me all that.

So I said, 'That's enough bollocks. I want you to move and fuck off now. You're boring me, fuck off.'

With that he replies, 'You wouldn't be sayin' that if you didn't have all your mates behind you,' referring to the other doormen.

'I'll tell you what,' I said. 'I don't need me mates behind me. Go round the back into the car park and I'll meet you there in two minutes.'

The other doormen had heard a lot of this and, as the guy moved round to the back, they started bursting out laughin'. They must have guessed what was coming.

I went round to the car park. I said, 'OK, you've been givin' it to me all night ...' and as I was talking to him, I hit him straight in the face. He went down, so I dragged him along the floor face down over these gravel stones and through some mud.

'Now are you happy?' I said. 'You've got what you deserved, now fuck off.' He managed to drag himself into a cab and away he went and I thought that was the last I'd see of him.

But the next day he came up to the Bodywise gym and apologised for his behaviour. He had been working up north somewhere where he was a head doorman and had heard about this guy named Stilks so he decided to see how fuckin' hard I really was. His idea was to try and do me out of my job.

When he found he'd taken on more than he could fuckin' well handle, he had the decency to come looking for me and apologise. That's the sign of a gentleman.

A few years later, I ran into him again when I started working on the doors in the City. The guy who was sent to pick me up and take me there turned out to be him, a bloke named Jamie. He was embarrassed at the time, but he turned out to be a good bloke in the end. He had been around a bit. He had worked for Dave Courtney and held a gun for him for some time and all that rubbish. But I'm glad he wasn't packing one on the night I ran into him, or I wouldn't have been able to serve him up quite as tasty as I did.

* * *

It was the fuckin' relentless savagery at Stars that was starting to take its toll on everyone.

Lots of people think that because doormen are big, hard bastards, they must be constantly looking for trouble. Yet nothin' could be further from the truth. All we really wanted was a quiet time, but that was the last thing we were getting. Every night – every fuckin' night, I swear it – there was an incident going on at that place. Stabbings had become commonplace, the club was awash with pills like Ecstasy and we were throwing out the scum left, right and centre.

By this time, even Sheena was noticing the change that was taking place in me. I was hyped up all the time, coming home at all hours with blood on my clothes. I'll tell ya, the fuckin' dry cleaning bills for blood-splattered jackets was mounting to ridiculous levels.

'Stellarg, I know it's your work and all that, but, honestly, I think you should slow down or you're gonna crack up,' she said once. 'Look at you. You never seem to be sleeping and you're always in a mess. I don't know how all this is going to end.'

'Don't worry, love, I'm perfectly all right. I have no fucking intention of slowing down. It's just that things are a bit out of hand down the club and we are having to be a bit extra tough on the ones that misbehave, that's all.

'Well, as long as that's all,' she said. 'As long as you're not up to anything you shouldn't be doing.'

'Nah, don't worry, darling. I'm fine, I really am.'

But I wasn't. I was rapidly spinnin' out of fuckin' control. I knew my fists could still look after me when it came to it, when somethin' went off and it really mattered. But I seemed to be just lurchin' from one day to the next, from one sniff of coke to the next one. All the doormen were gettin' like it down at Stars. The place was starting to fuck us over big time.

And one night it came to a head. I had just thrown some swaggering bastard out and I got back into the club. Dave took one look at me and says, 'Bloody hell, Stilks, you look like shit.'

I was so exhausted from sniffing the coke, I had been taking more and more to get over the tiredness.

'It's all right,' I said to Dave. 'You take over the main duty on the door and I'll go up to the balcony and take it a bit easy up there. I'll just watch the bastards, make sure they don't get out of line.'

Well, I just about managed to get up to the balcony when everything started to go spinning round and round … and all I could hear was the faint sound of something that was familiar, something I knew from deep down, but I couldn't place it. The sound was getting louder and louder. It was the sound of that old sewing machine.

I put my hands to my head and started squeezing as hard

as I could. I had my hands over my ears, I was trying to block out the sound. But it wasn't coming from outside, it was coming from inside my fuckin' head.

I could feel myself going under. I could feel the waves washing over me again like they'd done when I was a kid in Cyprus. I was clinging on, I was fightin' it, but I knew I wasn't gonna win. And then that feelin' came again, that great feelin', the great *WHOOSH*! And then I slumped to the floor.

8

BYE-BYE, CHARLIE

WHEN YOU'RE BROKE RAISE YOUR PRICE.
STILKS

I AWOKE TO WHAT SOUNDED LIKE A BLOODY STAMPEDE OF ELEPHANTS COMIN' IN ME HOUSE. WHAT THE FUCK'S GOIN' ON? BUT I REALISE IT BEFORE I EVEN THINK IT. SOMEWHERE ALONG THE LINE, SOMEONE'S GOT THE WRONG IDEA AND THEY'VE GRASSED ME UP TO THE OLD BILL AS A DRUG-DEALER OR SOMETHING. BUT WHATEVER IT WAS, SOMEONE HAD HAD ENOUGH OF ME. I WAS IN BED, THE HOUSE WAS EMPTY 'COS WE WERE DOIN' IT UP AS USUAL, AND THERE WAS NOTHING IN THE HOUSE. ME AND SHEENA AND THE KIDS WERE SLEEPING ON MATTRESSES AND IT WAS SIX O'CLOCK IN THE MORNING. WHAT KIND OF A BLOODY DAWN CHORUS WAS THIS? THE CAT WAS TERRIFIED AND RAN AS FAST AS IT COULD FROM THE LIVING ROOM OUT THE BACK DOOR, SCREECHING AS IT WENT.

'Stop or I'll shoot,' shouted one of the CID. I thought, Christ, they're after the cat as well.

I sat up in bed, while these heavy coppers charged up the stairs into the bedroom.

I said, 'Hold up, we're fucking naked, give us a chance!'

'Don't move,' said one of 'em waving a piece of paper. 'We've got a warrant to search your place for illegal substances under the Dangerous Drugs Act.'

With that they handcuffed me, put me on the floor, stood on my back and told me to 'Stay down'.

Sheena and the kids got dressed and then they took me downstairs and started searching the house. I knew there was nothing in the house because I don't sell drugs, never have done and never want to. I would never bring drugs into the house. The cocaine was something I used for my own recreation and, anyway, since I heard the sewing machine again at Stars, I had been determined to give it up. My little experiment with sniffing coke was fucking well over.

So I offered the police a cup of tea, and this CID bloke, who I had never met, said, 'Look, these other CID guys are from out of the borough. They've come in from Greenwich. If it was down to us, we wouldn't bother you. We know of you, Stilks, and we know you don't deal drugs or anything like that. But these officers are not from our patch.'

That's when I realised it had to be something to do with Stars.

The local copper gave me the nod. 'We know you are no goody-goody Stilks, but if I was you I'd go round the house with these guys while they search it, if you know what I mean.'

I thought, Why? but then I sussed – given half a chance, they were fuckin' goin' to plant something.

So I decided I wouldn't let 'em outta my sight, however long they stayed in the house.

'Go on, go ahead,' I said to one of the coppers from Greenwich. 'Have a good look round. You'll find none of your so-called illegal substances here. Have a bloody good look. In fact, let me show you round.'

'That won't be necessary, sir,' said one of them. 'We can find our own way round.'

'But I insist.'

And with that I followed them round the lounge while they opened every fucking drawer, and even started tapping the floor to see if there were loose floorboards.

Then they pulled up a couple of the floorboards and underneath there's this huge 10ft drop.

'Plenty of space to hide somethin' there,' I said. And with that, one of 'em looked at me and called for the dog handler. This bloody great dog jumped down the hole practically dragging the handler with him. There was the dog sniffing around under the floor, but, of course, he didn't find anything 'cos there was nothing to find.

'Come upstairs if you want, that'll be easier. There's bugger all furniture except for a few mattresses and there's no carpet to speak of. You'll find it easier up there.'

And all this said with a pleasant smile. But I wasn't gonna

let these geezers out of my sight, whatever happened. They looked around the bathroom, removed the top of the cistern, and tapped the panelling on the bath.

'Nice suite, don't ya think?' I said. 'Wife chose it, she's always liked Aztec Yellow. Pleasing on the eye. And before you ask, no, those taps are not real gold.'

'Really, sir, we can manage on our own.'

'Don't be silly, I've told ya. I insist.'

They had a look in the bedrooms and then it was back downstairs to the kitchen. But I could see they were starting to flag. I insisted on pulling out the washing machine, which we had only just had plumbed in, so they could see behind it.

'Now what about the U-bend under the sink?' I said. 'I could probably get that off for ya if you want to roll up your sleeves and give me a hand. No? Then look, there's the garden. Let me show you.' And with that, I herded them outside. We've got quite a large garden but at that time it was a mess and really needed sorting out.

'You could probably hide tons of illegal substances out here,' I said. Then I handed them a spade and fork that were lying nearby. 'Here you go,' I said. 'Grab hold of these. I'd start at the bottom part if I were you. I'd do it meself only it's me back. But please be my guest and dig my garden. You never know what you might find. And I want it done thoroughly and properly. I'll be standing just here in case you need any advice … Oh yeah, and if you're not busy at the weekend, how about popping back and making sure it's all laid to lawn?'

Needless to say, they didn't stay much longer, but they did say they would be back.

After they'd gone, I phoned up Dave Bowdery and said, 'You ain't gonna fuckin' believe this, Dave, but I've just had me door kicked in by the Old Bill over some sort of drugs thing.'

There's a tiny pause, and Dave says, 'So have I. And they've threatened to come back with some bloody sniffer dog.'

'Well, that'd probably be the dog that's been round my house,' I said.

Later, another friend of ours told us he had had his door kicked in as well.

From there, Dave and I went down the dogs, 'cos that's what we do on a Thursday afternoon and – Old Bill or not – we was still gonna continue with our bit of fun.

Down at the track, I looked over and … fuck me, I turned to Dave, 'I recognise those two over there,' I said.

'Where?'

'Them two, leaning by that fence. Weren't they the two CID that questioned us about that stabbing in the toilets at Stars the other week?'

'You're fucking right.'

'I tell ya, Dave, they're following us.'

'Don't be stupid. You're just getting paranoid.'

'Well, I'll tell ya what we'll do then. We'll drive to a fuckin' dead-end road and see if they come after us. Let's go.'

So we jumped in the car. The police stayed at the track but I wasn't worried about that because I was sure some others would pick up our trail. So we headed down to the marshes; there was only one way in and one way out.

We parked up and, sure enough, another car followed us in and had nowhere to go, so turned round and was gone.

When the word got round, most of my mates told me I was mad and in the grip of paranoia.

'I ain't got paranoia,' I'd say. 'They're following us, I know they are.'

A few days later, I was lying in bed with Sheena and the wife goes, 'I can hear something in the loft.'

'Don't be fuckin' stupid.'

'I'm telling you, there's someone in the loft, Stellarg,' said Sheena. 'Look! Did you just see that flash?'

'What flash?'

She goes, 'That one, look, there in the corner of the room. There it is again.'

That was enough for me. I was straight out of bed and examining the room. They had drilled minute holes for fibre optics into the room and the flash was where they were taking photographs of us. They said they'd be back, but I never thought it would be anything like this.

I've told people this since and no one has bloody well believed me. The usual answer is, 'Nah, Stilks, it's you. You've been sniffing that fucking coke for too long.'

But I was sure it wasn't me and so I went and told the whole story to a solicitor so that I could get it all down on record. They were definitely taking photographs using fibre optics. This completely freaked out Sheena who phoned the police.

Within 15 seconds, a troop of Old Bill came running into the house and I thought, What the fuck's happenin'? I swear on my life I never asked them to check the loft. But they ran upstairs and I saw one man go into the loft. But seconds later I saw *two* men come out. The second one was all wired up, and had things all round him.

I went, 'Hold up, there's two of you come out of there.'

But one of the Old Bill replied, 'No, there's no one up there, mate, there's no one in your loft, you're imagining things.'

The whole road had been blocked off when the police arrived, and now here they were calmly telling me nothing had fuckin' happened. They all got back in their cars and off they went.

I didn't know what the fuck to do. If I made a complaint to the Old Bill they would laugh, they weren't gonna take no complaint off me. So I went back to the solicitor and told him the whole thing and made a complete statement. So it was down on record and, touch wood, I haven't had any more trouble from them.

But I think it was because they were out-of-town CID from Greenwich that were put on me, and had come from another borough and didn't get an arrest. I reckon the Bexley lot gave them a bollocking: 'What you doin' coming down our patch? We know who's who and who's doin' what.' So the Greenwich lot decided to do it secretly. They were determined to get something on me, so they could go back with a result and put two fingers up to the local blokes.

But by then I had cleaned up my drug habit totally. I was still working down at Stars, and the place was turning into a right fucking hell-hole but I was no longer sniffing. I'd learned my lesson. It wasn't just that bloody sewing machine, although that was the final fucking straw, but it was the fact me and Dave could never leave the stuff alone.

I realised it was bad when we were driving home from Stars at about 3.30 in the morning and Dave goes, 'Do you fancy another little bit?'

And I say, 'Yeah, don't mind.'

He knew a place that was open 24 hours so we got over there, knocked on the door and went in. This bloke kept the stuff in a bloody great pepper pot. He shook some out, we did it, and I immediately felt like shit. I went home and the next morning I still felt like shit, so I thought, What the fuck am I doin' this for? So straight away I decided to give it up and, I tell ya, it ain't easy but it can be done, and it can be done quite quickly.

First, I cut out a couple of days a week and, when I'd adjusted to that, I didn't do it at all during the week, only on weekends. I then cut down the amount I did on weekends. People in the toilet at Stars sniffing it up? I couldn't be fucking bothered, just left 'em alone to get on with it. If anyone said, 'Shall we go and raid 'em?' I'd say, 'Nah, it's all fucking shit anyway.'

Eventually, I got it down to one day a week and I was sleeping better, training better, looking healthier, me brain was working faster, and I even felt like starting up a new business again. I wanted to get back on the right track and earn meself money. And before I realised it, I found the drug that I liked most of all – a good night's sleep!

I came off coke quite quickly and I know I'll never touch the stuff again. But then I am a very strong-willed person. I don't smoke or drink. Some people might find it hard giving up a habit like sniffing coke, and I don't wanna sound like I'm moralising here, but I've discovered that life without it is even more energetic than when you're on it. Only this time, I'm in control. As I say, I was an adult when I tried it and I never had anything to do with selling it or passing it on. And, yeah, I've seen people go fucking mad on the stuff. Most of my mates thought that when I was bugged by the Old Bill, it was all only in me head because of the amount of coke I'd sniffed.

Giving up cocaine is hard but it's worth it. You get more respect by saying 'no' than just giving in and ending up a druggie who can't even be bothered to get out of bed and go to work. And it can screw your head up. I once charged into a crowd at Stars screaming, 'I'm gonna fuckin' do ya,' thinking there was a fight goin' on, until Dave had to restrain me. I was sure I'd seen somethin', but there was nothin' goin' on, it was all in me 'ead.

But now I was clean and all I wanted to do was make a bit of money. Bodywise had been doin' all right but it wasn't the major earner I knew it could be, so when one of the lads had the idea of hiring the gym, I thought it was a good idea.

'What you gonna use it for?' I asked.

'I wanna do a bit of a rave, 'cos where I do 'em, at the Squash Club in Welling, we've been banned.'

'Well, what's in it for me?'

He says, 'I'll put a bit of a bar up and we'll sell drinks. It's a fiver on the door so I should earn good money and I'll give you a grand.'

It was tempting. He wanted me to supply the doormen and move all the gym gear out of the way.

The night of the rave arrives, and there's loads of people turning up, a really good night. At the end, about 4.00am, I got the music turned off and started ushering them out. Some of them were customers to my gym so I didn't want to upset them. We weren't Stars, so I didn't want to beat everyone up. I wanted to come across as likeable and do everything in a gentle manner.

But there was this group of four boys, big lumps, who I recognised from over the Plough. I told them we wanted to sweep up and get all the gym machines back in place. I wasn't trying to be too aggressive because they were local lads I knew on a daily basis. But they refused to fucking leave so I said, 'I've had enough, lads. Now off you go, you're goin' down the stairs.'

I took 'em down there and let them finish their drinks outside. It was now about 5.00am. I was taking all the rubbish out and they were still there and starin' at me as if I was a cunt. I couldn't be doin' with it and took no notice of 'em until one of them flicked his cigarette butt at me.

That was it, 'You obviously want it,' I said to them. 'You've been hangin' about all night, I don't know what for, but you obviously want it.'

There was me, Dave Bowdery, Tony Ward and Matt. Four of us, four of them.

I went over to the first one, jumped on top of him, and hit him while I was sittin' on him. I hit him about ten times in the face. He had a detached retina later.

Then I stood him up, put me arm round him, walked him down the road and said, 'If you want some more during the week, just come down and I'll give you some fuckin' more.'

While that was going on, one of the others tried to have a go. Matt hits him and he's gone over. Another one of the yobs says, 'I'll have some of that,' and starts shaping up as if he's a bit of a boxer. So Dave, who's got the hardest right hand in the business, remember, goes, 'Oh lovely, I like a bit of sport.' He ducks and dives, the bloke's thrown two and missed and Dave just hits him once and he's over on his arse. That was the end of him. The other one ran off. They were all beaten.

We went off home, but there was something in my head. I said to Sheena, 'Somethin' ain't right. I want to drive back past the gym and have a look.'

And, sure enough, it weren't right. They'd put me fuckin' windows through! They'd thrown bricks through all the windows; I couldn't fucking believe it. I was looking up and down the road and saw the dustbin men over the road. I said, 'Oi, lads, did you see who done this?' And they had, and knew where the bastards had gone and what van they'd used. They pointed. So I went up there and spotted the van. Then I rounded up Tony Ward and a friend of mine named Jeff. By this time, it was 8.00am. I needed Tony and Jeff just in case the geezers had a bit of a back-up, like a couple of brothers.

We went round to one guy's house and his mum answered the door.

'Your son's smashed me windows. I wanna see him, where is he?'

'He's out, he ain't here, he went to a party,' she said.

'Yeah I know, it was my party. He was in such a fuckin' party mood he put me windows through. Now I want compensation.'

'My son wouldn't do anything like that. But you'd better come in and sit down.'

First, she accused me of threatening her and wanted to call the police, which was OK by me. Then she said she'd try and phone her son, but she didn't. In the end, I said, 'I'll tell ya what I'm going to do. I'll go back and start cleaning up the shit in my gym. I've had a look at the windows and I reckon there's about £300 worth of damage. If I don't have £300 at my gym by 2.00pm, you will leave me no choice but to come back to your house and put your windows through. Do I make myself clear? It ain't something I want to do, but it's something I will have to do. Have you got the message?'

'I'm going to phone the police. You are threatening me,' she said.

'You do what you have to do.' I replied. 'But if that £300 is not there by 2.00pm I will be back here.'

Come 2.00pm, it was all there in nice crisp fifties.

* * *

Now I was drug-free, I wanted the lot. More work. I wasn't that interested in the rabble going down Stars any more, I was looking for anything extra I could take on. And then Mark Rowe, who I went to Galleon's Mount Infants with, said he was in the fight game looking after security. He now manages Julius Francis, but in those days he was involved in the fight between Chris Eubank and Michael Watson, north of the river.

He phones me up and asks whether I want to look after the boxers. I thought, Not really, especially when he told me the money wasn't very much.

But he said, 'Come on, Stilks, you'll get to see all the big fights from the ringside, seats worth two or three hundred quid, and some of the fights are world title bouts.'

I thought about it and replied, 'Doesn't sound too bad. Can I bring a friend?'

'If you want.'

And that's how me and Lindon Pusey, who was also at Stars, happened to start going to these fights. We'd even miss a few Saturdays at the club if it was for a good scrap. And that's how we both happened to be going to White Hart Lane in Tottenham on 21 September 1991. Our job was to stick closely to Chris Eubank and make sure he wasn't harmed. At the time, Eubank was a winner and, for some strange reason, the British don't like winners. Michael Watson was from Islington, down the road from Tottenham, and a local boy. The crowd was very much on his side.

As me and Lindon went into the stadium, you could sense the bloody tension and electricity in the air.

It was a re-match and they were fighting for the WBO World Super-Middleweight Championship. They'd met earlier in the year at Earl's Court, when Eubank had narrowly won and Watson had been accused of being too defensive. It was Michael's third and possibly his last attempt to grab a world title, and it seemed like the whole of the bleedin' crowd was on his side.

'Wow,' I say to Lindon. 'If Michael doesn't pull this one off, there could be a bit of trouble here, mate. If this lot gets angry, they could smash the place up easily.'

Eubank was seen by the crowd to be arrogant and, because he was from Brighton and not a local lad, they hated him. A handful of us were picked to stay really close to Chris, wait outside his dressing room and make sure no one got in. When he came out to go to the ring, we were right in close beside him so no one could have a go or anything like that. I was stuck to him like fuckin' glue right the way into the ring.

The place was electric. I had to keep looking round all the time, eyes constantly darting across the arena looking for trouble. Mark Parish turned up and said, 'Come with me,

Stilksy, you're down at the ringside.' A couple of my friends, who were well into boxing, had also turned up and joined me and Lindon down there, front fucking row.

'Bloody hell, Stilks,' said Mark, 'they're like animals in here,' and he was right, the shouting and screaming was deafening and there were small skirmishes breaking out here and there. Nothing big, though, and nothing that wasn't quickly defused. Nothing that needed our attention anyway.

The lights were beaming down on the ring, and then the bell went. It was the signal for pandemonium.

Watson came out from the beginning carrying the fight to Eubank. He was fighting at a heavier weight, about 12st I think, than at the Earl's Court fight and he was also going at a faster pace. Michael looked determined to win the fight and was throwing every punch he could think of in an effort to get it over with as quickly as possible.

The crowd were roaring him on. Watson was stalking Eubank and picking him off with a flurry of fast shots. Eubank, who usually likes to throw long-range counters, was given no time at all to find a rhythm. This looked like Michael's fight all the way and the punters were going delirious.

I turned to Lindon. 'Don't look so worried, mate. Watson looks like he's got this one sewn up. This lot will go away happy. The last thing they'll want to do is fight.'

Michael was blocking Eubank's shots on his gloves. It looked like the undefeated dandy from the south coast had met his match at last in Watson, who was about 26 years old at the time. All the first few rounds went to Watson easily but, by about the seventh or eighth, I noticed Michael's higher work rate was becoming more difficult to sustain. Eubank's power was beginning to tell.

But by the ninth, Michael was back in charge and I think he took the tenth as well.

The eleventh turned out to be the deciding round. In the opening minute, Eubank had Watson retreating to the ropes where he swayed out of range before Michael regained the centre of the ring. Fuck the crowd, I thought by now. I couldn't take my eyes off the fight in front of me. I didn't wanna know about anything goin' on around me. Eubank seemed spent and then two short stiff rights from Watson, and the undefeated boxer dropped on to one knee. The crowd went fucking ballistic, there are no words to describe it. I've never known anything like it. They went bloody nuts. Screamin', shoutin', hollerin' at the top of their voices. Chants of 'WATSON, WATSON' were picked up with everyone stampin' and bangin' whatever they could get their hands on. It was the first time Chris had even taken a count, and when I glanced into his corner I thought, They don't look very happy. But the crowd was delirious.

Eubank took a standing count of eight and then walked to a neutral corner. He was one mad fucker. And before anyone knew what was going on, he went straight for Watson and hit him twice – a right uppercut and a left hook.

Thankfully, the bell rang. I didn't know how anyone could have taken those two mighty blows but Michael made it to his corner and assured them he was all right. But I wasn't so sure and neither were his seconds.

Ding! Round 12. Michael came out with his arms down and I thought, Oh God, no! I screamed, 'Get your arms up, Michael, for fuck's sake get your arms up.' And then the referee Roy Francis ordered both the fighters to touch gloves as is traditional for the last round.

'Lindon, Lindon,' I shouted to my mate. 'They've go to stop it. Watson's gonna be killed.' I was almost in tears. It was like watching a bleedin' train crash about to happen and not being able to do anything about it. I looked at the ref and tried to will him to stop what was going to happen. But he didn't. It went on for another 29 seconds; 29 seconds of two-fisted fury from Eubank before Francis called a halt to the fight and Michael slumped unconscious to the ground.

What happened next was nothing short of anarchy and bedlam. I'd seen it go off fucking hundreds of times, but nothin', nothin' in my life, had prepared me for what happened at White Hart Lane.

Everyone, all 15,000 of them, were on their feet and it looked like the fucking majority were making their way to the ring. Fights were breaking out all over the place and Michael's supporters from 100 yards away ran to the ring thinking the end was premature.

That's when I managed to get a look at the marking of the three ringside judges. All three of them had Watson leading Eubank by one, two and, in the case of the Puerto Rican judge, Nelson Vasquez, by four rounds. His supporters couldn't believe it had been stopped. But they hadn't been in the £250 seats like me and Lindon. They hadn't seen the poor bastard come out for that twelfth round. He didn't know where the fuck he was. I don't know about stopping it prematurely – it should have been bleedin' well stopped a lot earlier.

'Stilks, get in the fucking ring, try and get some order in there,' shouted Mark who was running the security. The ring was packed and poor old Michael was lying collapsed on the canvas. 'Where the fuck's the doctor? Where's the stretcher?' everyone was shouting. Bloody National Health Service, I thought. But the crowds in and out of the ring were so big that neither the doctor nor the stretcher could get there, and the time was slipping away … one minute … two … three … still no doctor!

No one knew how badly Michael was knocked out, we were all praying a bit of smelling salts would bring him through. But as the time got longer, everyone was starting to panic. Where the fuck was the doctor? More of Eubank's people were trying to get into the ring to celebrate his winning and no one was giving Watson any room. The crowds were still preventing medical help getting through, and everyone feared then that something serious had happened and the delay was making it much, much worse. This wasn't a normal knock down. Mark shouts, 'I'll try and get some people out of the ring. You, Stilks, prevent anyone else from getting in, doesn't matter who the fuck they are.'

'Right.'

And so I went at it. I was standing at the corner of the ring when this well-dressed black guy comes over and steps up to get in the ring.

'Sorry, mate, that's it, no more in the ring. We're tryin' to get 'em out.'

'I'm getting in the ring.'

'No, you're not, mate, you ain't going nowhere.'

'But I'm Chris Eubank's brother, Simon.'

'I don't give a fuck who you are. Say what you like, you ain't getting' in.'

And with that I pushed him and he went flying over.

Then it started. All the blacks had picked up chairs because Simon had gone over, and they started throwing them at me. I'm dodging chairs, pushing blokes, trying to protect me head. And there's Michael still in the ring out cold.

Then there was a bit of luck. Nigel Benn, who was WBO Middleweight Champion at the time, came runnin' round from the other side. I thought, Thank God, the Dark Destroyer himself is here. And he started appealing to the crowd to stop throwing the chairs. 'Stop, stop,' he was shouting. 'Michael's still in there and you are making things worse.' They all recognised who he was and, luckily, Nigel Benn managed to quieten them down.

With that, Mark called me over and said we'd got to get Chris Eubank out of the ring. By now, everyone knew something had happened to Watson but no one knew what and still no doctor had turned up. But if they didn't know what had happened to Michael, they knew who to blame –

Chris Eubank. You could see the fear in Eubank's face. He was shitting himself about what the crowd would do to him.

'Get him out of the ring, get him out of sight,' barked Mark. 'If it's not done now, we are set for a full-scale fucking riot.'

It looked an impossible task, we couldn't just hold Chris's hand and escort him away, so I came up with a plan. I got about five of us together.

'Right,' I said. 'Everyone get into a sort of rugby scrum, only standing up. Interlock arms and head down. You, Chris – get down here and in the middle of the scrum where no one can see ya. Right now, let's go.'

And slowly we walked and inched our way along. Some blows were raining down on us but we were taking it across the shoulders, and Eubank was perfectly protected in the middle of the scrum. They were spittin' at us, punchin' us, kickin' us all the way from the ring back down to the dressing room. It was a frightening night.

When we got Chris safely in his room, I said to Lindon Pusey, 'Let's get the fuck out of here.' And as we were moving down the corridor, I saw this stretcher with Michael Watson on it. Finally, they had managed to get the poor bloke out of the ring. But it had taken an agonising seven minutes before the British Boxing Board of Control doctor had managed to get to Watson's side in the ring. But that was little compensation for Michael. He was in a coma, suffered serious brain damage and underwent surgery to remove a blood clot. He had gone without treatment and oxygen for too long after his collapse.

In fact, Michael didn't receive oxygen for 30 minutes and it was two hours before he was wheeled into an operating theatre. He has made a remarkable recovery for someone who most medical experts said would never get better and he has been awarded damages from the Boxing Board. It was ruled he would have made a good recovery if the doctor had been able to enter the ring immediately and emergency equipment and experienced medics had been present.

That's all fuckin' well and good, and I don't think anyone would begrudge Watson a penny of his massive settlement. He still needs help to walk and he struggles with his memory. But I still reckon the bout should have been stopped at the end of the eleventh, regardless of the consequences.

As me and Lindon made our way back south of the river, I thought what bleedin' chaos the whole evening had descended into. And yet if Michael Watson had got up off that canvas, how different it all would have been.

Mark used us at quite a few other fights, mainly at the Royal Albert Hall. He used to make us put these red steward sweatshirts on so he would know where we were around the place.

We'd ask him where he wanted us to stand and then, as soon as he was out of sight, we'd whip off the red sweatshirts, go and find two nice seats, sit down, watch a nice evening of boxing and, at the end of the night, put the sweatshirts back on.

Then we'd walk back down to Mark, hold out our hands and get paid for it. This went on for a good 12 fights until

Mark caught on and then he sacked us, so it was back to Stars.

The difference between Stars and the Royal Albert Hall was incredible. Even the fuckin' Wild West was tamer than the animals at that club. It had started off so nicely a couple of years earlier, and now it was like a garbage pit for the seediest mugs and thugs to hang out in.

Loads of times, I thought about jacking it in, me heart just wasn't in it any more. The thing about being a doorman is that you like to keep an orderly house. If things run smoothly, everyone has a lot of fun. The punters get a late drink and a good dance or whatever, and we all have an easier time. Knocking scum out is OK. But it's much better when you don't have to do it.

At Stars there was no alternative. I had broken my hand so many times I was wonderin' if it might not fuckin' shatter the next time I had to give someone a good straightener. But I always had me Stilks Strangle to fall back on and I was using it more and more as time went on.

The Bodywise gym had been doing all right, but I thought it was time to move on from that as well. I needed some money in the bank. With four young kids you never know what's going to crop up, so I needed a bit of cash for emergencies. That's how I came to sell the place.

About the only bloody good thing that happened towards the end of Stars was when I ran into this young fella named Matt Smith. He was only about 18 or 19 and had been coming in a few weeks. Me and Dave had been keepin' an eye on him, 'cos he always bowled around head up, shoulders back, as if he owned the place. And if there was a punch-up, he always seemed to be involved.

So I said to Dave, 'Keep an eye on him, and if he gets involved again we'll double up on him and have him out.'

A couple of hours later, there's this geezer down the bottom of the stairs rolling up a joint. So I walked down and told him, 'Listen, mate, you ain't gonna smoke that in here.'

'Nah, of course not,' he replies.

But 20 minutes later, someone said they could smell it, and I saw this same fella hiding a joint. Another five minutes and he looks up at me and takes a drag. I thought, He's takin' the piss.

So I went back downstairs, even though me hand was broken again at the time from the night before.

I said, 'Listen, mate, I've told you before, no puffin' in here.'

With that, he goes to throw a left hook at me, and I went into one of me judo throws and threw him straight down on the floor, put me knee on his chest, drew me right hand back and said, 'It's your lucky night. I ain't gonna knock you out because me hand's broken.' And then I dragged him off the floor.

As soon as I did that, I heard *bang*! and I've looked behind me and it's this fella Matt Smith.

'Whaddya do that for?' I said.

'I heard you said you were gonna knock him out but you couldn't because of your hand. So I thought I'd do it for you.'

After that, Matt became a great friend and he still is.

But each week the number of punters going to Stars was dropping. The place was getting worse and the only people left going there were drug-dealers and fucking idiots. The place was getting rougher but Keith Brown was cutting down on the number of doormen. It went from 16 to 12 and then down to 10. A year later, it was eight and then we were down to six, and we all knew we were coming to the end of Stars. It was just a matter of time.

There were about 500 people going through the door at this time, as opposed to the 2,000 or so that were there when it opened. By the time it got down to four doormen, even though they were paying us good money, I had to have a word with the manager.

I said, 'Look, this place is fucking rough, mate, and there ain't enough of us here any more to handle this.'

'Don't worry, Stilks, I'm right behind you.' He was a big lump, Keith Brown, a good 20st. But he wasn't really there to support us. There were just the four of us on the door greeting, and a house full of nutters inside.

One bloke comes out and shouts, 'Hurry up, there's some bloke been beat up inside.'

We go running in to find this geezer who had had the fucking shit kicked out of him. He was bleeding from everywhere having been kicked in the ribs; he was in a terrible way. So we carried him back out to the reception and put him down. He had teeth missing and gashes in his face.

So I turned to the manager and said, 'Look at him, just look at him. This is your fucking fault. The reason this geezer is hurt like this is because you've deliberately cut down on the fucking doormen. I told you it can't be controlled with fucking four men.'

And with that – *bang*! – I hit Keith Brown on the chin. He went back, and I said to Dave Bowdery, 'Come on, Dave, we're going home.' And that was the end of Stars for me after three of the wildest years of my life.

One month later, the club was shut down.

9

CITY SLICKER

OTHER PEOPLE'S SAFETY MUST COME BEFORE YOUR OWN.
STILKS

'**W**ELL, DON'T THINK YOU'RE GOING TO BE SITTING AROUND ALL DAY AND NIGHT, STELLARG,' SAID SHEENA. 'YOU CAN MAKE YOURSELF USEFUL.'

I thought I *had* been making myself useful; I'd got four kids by now! And they were all beautiful girls.

'And you can start by helping look after the kids,' said Sheena.

Louise, my youngest then, had just started going to nursery. Sheena was busy with the three elder ones, 'cos they were still young. She was washin', ironin', cookin' and all the rest of it. So I think, OK, Sheen, I'll give it a go. So I say to her, 'How can I help?'

'The least you can do is pick up Louise from her pre-school place. That would be a big help because picking her up breaks up my day. And if you're any good at it, you can start taking her there in the morning as well.'

I thought, That's fine, if that's me job, that's me job.

'Don't worry, love, it's easy,' I said.

'Yeah, well, just make sure you don't embarrass me in front of any other mums, that's the only thing.'

So I was helpin' out, doin' me bit, and one day I went round to the school to pick Louise up. It was fucking raining so I got there early and parked right outside the school. I went and got Louise and put her in the car and the rain was really pissin' down hard, and I couldn't really see anything. Everything was misted up, I couldn't see out of the back window of the car. I thought what I'd do was pull out gently, not really looking but take it easy so anyone behind was aware of what was going on.

The school was on a main road in Bexleyheath, and there I was slowly pulling out while a lorry was approaching from the opposite direction, taking up the whole of the oncoming lane. Next thing I know as I pull out, this car comes down the side, hits me, bounces off and scrapes the lorry. The driver in the car pulls over to the front and I thought, Oh lovely, I've got a claim here. He's just hit me from behind.

So I got out of the car to have a word with him and, as I do that, the geezer puts his foot down and drives off. So I got back in the car and started chasing him down the road. I was pressing the horn to try and get him to pull over and stop. But he's havin' none of it. I'm punching the horn like it's some toe-rag from Stars and Louise starts laughing. She thinks the beep-beep game is great fun.

The driver in front suddenly takes the first left and I quickly follow him. He's driving like a fuckin' lunatic and I'm driving like a lunatic. *Beep*! Me daughter's laughing. He has no intention of stopping and, by this time, I'm starting to get mad. Why the fuck doesn't he pull over? But instead he increases his speed and, at the next junction, turns left again. This has taken about three or four minutes and he has gone all round the bleedin' block. I'm on his tail

And then all of a sudden he has to stop, not 'cos he wants to, but because the car in front of him wants to turn right.

That's it, I seized my chance. I stopped right behind him and thought, Lovely, he's gonna get it now.

So I got out of the car, ran round and went to pull open his door … but he quickly locked it. His mate tried to get out the other side, and I shouted, 'You can sit back down or you'll fuckin' get it as well.' So he got back in but now both doors were locked, so I thought the only thing to do was get through the windscreen. So I jumped on the bonnet, the driver is screaming inside, and I'm trying to kick the windscreen in.

Just at that moment, the car in front completed the right turn and the driver accelerated, which threw me from the bonnet up on to the bloody roof of the car. I had no alternative but to scramble off on to the boot and jump off the car.

It was just at that moment I looked left and noticed where we were – we were just passing the school. The driver had gone all round the block. There were all these mums who had come to pick up their kids, little Joan and little John, looking at me with open mouths. Most of them were my neighbours and they had probably always suspected I was a bit of a lunatic. So I just looked at 'em, gave 'em a smile, and summoning up as much dignity as possible, cheerily said, 'Afternoon, ladies. I'll be picking up Louise again tomorrow. Have a nice day.'

When we got home, Sheena asked if everything had gone off all right.

'Yes, love, no problems whatsoever. Louise was as good as gold.'

That's when my daughter piped up, 'Mummy, Mummy, Daddy played this game with another man in his car. He kept pressing the beeper and the man had to drive off quickly. Daddy won because in the end he was standing on the other man's car as King of the Castle.'

Sheena just took one withering look at me and, without saying anything, very slowly started shaking her head.

* * *

She must have been very relieved when there was another knock on the door. This time it wasn't Chris Olley but a bloke named Keith Price, who I'd worked with at the Station.

He came straight to the point. 'Stilks, we need a doorman at Sahara's,' he said.

'What the fuck's Sahara's?'

'It's an over-30s singles club.'

'You're havin' a joke, ain'tcha, Keith?'

'Nah, you'll enjoy it, Stilksy mate.'

'I can't be doin' with that, really. Not bleedin' over-30s and single.'

'Stilks, you're getting' on now and you want a nice easy one. This is it, I'm telling you, this is it. It's somewhere where you can relax and you won't have to stress yourself out like you did back at Stars. It's somewhere where you can retire.'

So I thought, Fuckin' hell, one thing's for sure, I can't be sitting in weekends. It drives me mad. And I'll be able to get out a bit during the week and from under Sheena's feet.

'OK,' I said. 'Put me down.'

So I made it up to Sahara's, in Lewisham, South London, to have a look round. And there's people in there –30, 40, 50 and even some of 'em 60 years old. I'm scratchin' me head and I can't work it out. What are these people doin' in a nightclub? In all my years on the door, I had never seen people this old clubbing it. I was used to working with teenagers and young kids who were kicking off every ten minutes, raving it, dropping Es and generally getting out of their heads. Here was a club which played '70s and '80s music and I just couldn't work it out. As people were coming in, I was jumping down their throats, givin' 'em the old 'Let's-have-no-trouble' bollocks. There was a doorman there called Sid Brown and he was saying, 'Stilks, for Christ's sake, calm down, calm down. These ain't kids, these are grown-ups. If people can't behave at 30, they ain't never gonna behave. You've got to learn to relax. There's a way of doin' this thing.'

And, in fact, Sid is one of the best doormen I've ever met, especially when it comes to talking to people. He has a great manner about him. If you said, 'Look at her, she ain't half bloody ugly,' he would reply, 'They're all God's children, Stilks, they're all God's children.'

If I got mad and said, 'I'll do that cunt in a minute,' he would reply, 'Stop, that's someone's son, Stilks. Calm down.'

He would always try to put each situation into perspective and he taught me one of the great things in life – you don't have to hit 'em all to put sense into them. Some of them you can talk to.

Sahara's holds about 250, so it was tiny compared with Stars, and Keith Price told me that it didn't kick off very often but when it did kick off, it kicked off proper. They were grown men, it wasn't going to be as easy as just slapping about a couple of kids who thought they were hard.

The first incident happened when this geezer wanted to talk to the new doorman, who was me. But for the first couple of weeks, I wanted to be left alone to soak up the atmosphere and work out where all the pressure points might be in the club if it went off. When I'm needed in the club, I want to know where every type of person is in that club. That way, if it kicks off anywhere I know who it's probably gonna be before I get there.

For example, if you sit on a bus, the chances are you'll sit in the same seat. If you've got a pub you go to regularly, it's odds-on you'll be sitting on the same chair. People are creatures of habit and my skill at being a doorman is that I don't know names. But when you know faces, you know if they've been in before and if they've ever caused trouble. And if they walk into that club, I'll know exactly where they're gonna stand. That's why I always need a few weeks of soaking up the atmosphere and getting to know the faces. So if someone says, 'It's kicked off in the left-hand bar,' I'll probably know who the fucker is that caused it. That way, I know what I'm getting into before I even get there.

This bloke who wanted to talk to me was a bit of a Jack the Lad. He was quite big and he was walking round as if he owned the place. He looked mean and tough. When it all kicked off, this geezer was behind it. So I grabbed him and dragged him to the front door saying, 'I hear you wanted a word with me, well here's a couple for you – fuck off!'

But I was thinking, When I get him out of this front door, we are going to be on our own and he's going to throw a few wild ones at me and let me have it. He was a big, tough, hard nut. So I was winding meself up all the way to the front door and, when I got there, I pushed him up against the wall and gave him a couple in his chest. I pulled him down and *bang*! started throwing his head against the wall. I'd wound myself up so much thinking he looked tough when he swaggered about that I really laid into him. But whether it was adrenalin rush or whatever, he turned out to be like a rag doll.

His girlfriend, who recognised me, came running and shouting, 'Stilks, Stilks, stop, stop.' And I did stop, and was glad when they'd gone. But it goes to show that appearances can be deceptive and yet, as a doorman, you have to take things on face value because you are putting your own life on the line. Maybe I shouldn't have hit him so hard, but he had been menacing me, wanting to talk to me and then swaggering around the club.

But the only time I really regretted things was when I saw this bloke on the dance floor. There is a rule of 'no drinks' and 'no smoking' on the dance floor. It's for two reasons – if you spill a drink, someone's gonna slip over and hurt themselves. And if you're smoking, there are chances you'll burn someone else's coat or dress and then there'll be a punch-up over nothing.

So I went up to this fella who had a bottle of beer in his hand.

'Sorry, mate,' I said. 'No drinking and smoking on the dance floor.' I went over to the other side of the club to check a few things out and came back. He was still there.

'Look, mate, I've told you once and I won't tell you again, take your fucking bottle off the dance floor,' I said. He's still dancin' about and I thought, Maybe he ain't heard me.

So I shouted, 'Can you hear me, mate? Take your bottle off the dance floor.' I'd told him three times, and now I had to take the bottle off him. He was holding it in his left hand and I grabbed it. As I did that, he hit me in the chops with his right. I felt that, so I pulled the bottle off him, wound one back, right to the back, and let it go – *bang*! – and hit him straight on the chin. With that, he went backwards and landed on a pint glass on a table, which cut him badly across the hand.

He's come back at me and thrown another punch, and now there's blood everywhere. So I grabbed him in a hug and walked him over to the door. 'Look, mate, don't be fucking stupid. You've been an idiot on the dance floor, now you've cut yourself. Do yourself a favour, fuck off and get yourself sewn up.'

With that, he went downstairs, congealed blood everywhere, and phoned an ambulance.

Later, we heard that he had lost the feeling in two of his fingers, and tried to sue the club for compensation. But because I had done things in the correct professional manner by warning him a number of times, he didn't stand a chance.

But I do regret his injuries. You don't mind people getting a black eye or a few bruised ribs, but you don't like permanent injuries like that. If people go out for a night and misbehave, you don't want to kill 'em, just teach 'em a few manners. That geezer was unlucky falling on that pint glass; most of the people I hit get better and live to fight another day.

Remember, these are big guys now, not kids. And they can usually dish it out as well as take it.

I remember these two fellas, must have been in their late 30s, quite tall, quite big. They had been arguing at the bar with one of the barmaids over the price of a drink and she called us over.

I said to one of them, 'Excuse me, I'd like to speak to you at the door please.'

Once I got them both to the door, I said, 'Look, the barmaid doesn't want you in here, you're arguing all the time. You've gotta go, mate.'

'We're not goin',' says one of 'em. 'We're not leavin', we've paid to come in. If you want to throw us out, you'll have to give us our money back.'

I explained carefully, 'No, boys, no, you don't understand. I'm telling you, you will have to go.'

They kept on and on so I thought, Bollocks, and pushed one of 'em in the chest. He fell back about three steps and said, 'Right, that's it, I'm going to get the Old Bill and have you nicked for assault.'

'Gonna call the fuckin' police, are ya?'

'Yeah.'

I looked round and realised it was another doorman's – Sid's – birthday because someone had bought him a birthday cake. Sid was inside and I reckoned he wouldn't mind, so I picked up the cake and threw it at the geezer who was giving me all the fucking lip. It landed on his chest and slid down.

And I said, 'While you're up at the Old Bill, don't forget to tell 'em that I done you with a cake!'

* * *

Ever since the CID had refused to dig my garden and come back and re-lay it for me when they were looking for the 'illegal substances', I'd just let it go. It was about 10ft tall with bramble bushes, a few trees and low fences. You couldn't even get from one end to the other. It was a bloody jungle out there. Sheena was just about at the end of her tether with it.

'Stellarg,' she'd say. 'What are we going to do about the garden? Something has got to be done.'

'Leave that to me, love.'

I had a brilliant idea. So I went down to the local farm and I brought back two goats, a black one and a white one. I thought it was just what we needed to trim down the garden, so I decided to call them Black 'n' Decker.

Sheena went mad. 'They'll foul everywhere,' she said. 'The place will start to stink.'

'Nah, it won't, darling,' I replied. 'They only do little poohs, like guinea pigs, and they'll eat their way through the entire garden.'

So I put 'em out in the garden, peg 'em up, and there they are munching away at everything. And when they did shit they were only little droppings; it was just that there were a bloody lot of 'em!

I grew quite attached to Black 'n' Decker and I was going to keep them, but when they finished off my garden they decided they wanted to finish off the next-door neighbour's garden as well, and even the one after that. They took quite a shine to the rose bushes and everything, but the neighbours weren't too impressed.

Next-door there was a divorcée, a nice lady called

Madeleine, who had a daughter and a son. He was about 24 and she was about 18.

One day I got home about 3.00–4.00am, and the wife goes to me, 'Oh, they've had another party next-door. It's only just finished.'

The following week, she says the same, and this was going on for a few weeks, maybe a month or two.

Of course, it didn't bother me because, by the time I got in, it was all over.

I'd say to Sheena, 'Oh, for God's sake, leave the kids alone, they're only having a party. We have a party sometimes. I like to party.'

'Yeah, Stellarg, but you're not here while it's going on. It's bedlam.'

About this time, I had decided to give up on the Bloody National Health Service altogether. I needed yet another operation for the mastoiditis in me ear and this time I went privately. The Bloody National Health Service had been messing around with my ear long enough and it had never been a success. So I went to see Dr Bowdler down in Blackheath. I had the operation done and I was recuperating at home because I was in pain. I couldn't work down Sahara's while I was recovering, so I was at home at the weekends.

Anyway, it got to 10.00pm one Saturday night and the music next-door goes on, and it's fucking loud, especially for someone recovering from an ear operation.

I was trying to watch TV but the music next-door was

getting louder and louder and there were people coming all night.

'Don't worry, love,' says Sheena. 'This happens every week.'

Time goes on and it's 2.00am so I go round and ask them politely to turn it down.

They turn it down and we jump into bed. About half-an-hour later, they turn the music up and keep playing this one song over and over again.

I turn to Sheena, 'Look, love,' I said. 'Go next-door and tell them I've had enough, the party's over.'

She goes downstairs and knocks on the neighbours' door, but they haven't opened it.

'They are refusing to open the door, Stellarg,' she says to me exasperated.

'Look, love, I'm in pain. I have to get some sleep. Tell 'em to stop or I'm going to get fuckin' annoyed.'

But they still refused to open the door, so I got myself a pair of shorts, put my slippers on, and told Sheena to go down to the garden shed, which we had just had put up, and get me a hammer.

So here I am with half me head bandaged up like a mummy, wearing a pair of shorts and carpet slippers and holding a hammer in me hand. That's when I knocked on their door.

'Open the fucking door,' I shouted. I could see people in there so obviously they were taking the piss. I was getting right frustrated at being ignored. 'Open this fucking door,' I screamed. Nothing. So I looked round his front garden and he had all these gnomes there. 'ARRRRRRRGH!' I shouted as I grabbed the gnomes and started smashing them with the hammer. After I'd done all the gnomes in, I decided I might as well start on the front door itself.

So there I am smashin' the door panels with the fuckin' hammer when finally the door goes flying open and I'm in.

'Where's Alex, where is the cunt?' I shouted as I ran down the hall with the hammer in my hand. 'Where is he?' Everyone at the party is looking at me wide-eyed and open-mouthed. They can't believe it. Who let this madman in here?

Alex stands up in the hope of calming things and I scream, 'I fuckin' told you, you lunatic,' as I raised the hammer above me head and Alex cowers down trying to protect himself.

Just as I'm about to smash the fuck out of him, Nina, his sister, came up to me wearing this mini-skirt, grabs me by the arm and pleads, 'Stilks, don't hit him, don't hit him.'

I'm looking at her and I'm looking at him, who's now got his arms wrapped round his head expecting the worst, and go 'ARRRRRRRGH!' rush over to the stereo and smash that, hit the speakers as well … and there's this lovely silence.

'Alex,' I say, 'I want a word with you in the morning.'

The next day, he comes round at about 11.00am and apologises for the night before.

I said, 'Fucking sorry, are ya? Fucking sorry? I'll tell you, Alex, I don't mind a party, I like a party meself. But from now on you have two parties a year – one on your birthday and one at Christmas. And you can give me three days' notice beforehand so I ain't fucking in.'

That was the end of Alex's parties and it wasn't long afterwards they moved.

* * *

By now, I was really in my prime. I'd been working on the doors for a long time and I was fit and oozing confidence. I was full of meself, so when this girl at Sahara's came over to me and said these blokes were annoying her, she had come to the right man.

I walked over to them. I could see they were under 30 and shouldn't have been there. 'Look, lads,' I said. 'Don't talk to the girls, 'cos one of them is with someone and the other doesn't want to know.'

One of them then looks at me and says the immortal words every doorman has heard a thousand times – 'What you gonna do about it?'

With that, I hit him and he fell straight on to a table. He's out cold. The other one I grabbed, pulled him towards me and *bang*! hit him in the stomach. The third ran. With that I picked up a chair and held it above my head. I was waiting for the first one I'd knocked out to come round. He slowly started realising where he was, shaking his head a little. And with that I hit him over the head with the chair and knocked him out again.

That's when the manager came running over. 'Stilks, what are you doing?'

'Me job.'

'I know that, but you're supposed to prevent the club being smashed up, not do it yourself,' she laughed.

And then I looked round, one of the tables was over, a chair was broken and there were two customers lying out cold on the floor.

'Don't worry,' I said. 'I'll just throw 'em out and tidy up a bit.' I'd forgotten, this wasn't Stars where tables and chairs went flying every night. This was supposed to be a nice respectable club for the over-30s.

So I turned to the manageress and said, 'That's the kind of trouble you get when under-age drinkers are here. Better check the back door, I think they might be sneaking in.'

We were always trying to keep an eye out for who would make trouble and stop them getting in, but if they were determined, they would do it.

The ones we really had trouble with at the time were the Kosovan refugees. More and more of them were coming up every week and they were pests with the girls, pinching their bums. And they were always coming straight from the kebab shop and smelling like they hadn't washed for three months. But if they looked fairly respectable and they had the entrance money, there was not much we could do to keep them out. So we were always thinking of ways to turn them away.

We'd say things like, 'You ain't ironed your trousers' or 'Your shirt's the wrong colour.' What they used to do was go down the Oxfam shop and rob the bags of clothes that people had put outside to get a pair of trousers, 'cos most of them only had jeans.

One day, we had this bright idea to say to them, 'Terribly sorry, can you read and understand English?'

'Yes.'

'Do you know that sign? Do you know what 'Fire Exit' means?'

'Firey, Firey Excite,' they'd say.

'Sorry, mate. Can't come in. It's in the regulations. Unless you can clearly identify the exits in case of a fire and understand what is being communicated to you in English in case of a fire, then you can't come in. Sorry. It would be dangerous to let you in the club. We are doing this for your own sake, for your own fucking safety.'

We were always thinking up different reasons to keep them out, so naturally a lot of them would hang around outside.

One night, this girl passed out in the club and Keith Price, who was our top man at First Aid, did what he could for her and decided to take her downstairs for air, and walk her to her car.

So I took over the front door. Time was passing. It got to about three minutes and I thought to meself, What's happenin' here then? Keith had been down there a long time so I opened the door into the club and called Paul over.

'Hold on to the door, mate,' I said. 'Keith's been outside three minutes, dunno what's goin' on.'

So I ran out the front and I see Keith by this young lady's car. And he's surrounded by about eight of these Kosovans. They'd been hangin' around all night. I could see Keith was in trouble and thought I'd run back into the club and get the others and we'd take 'em on. But the Kosovans were getting closer and closer so I thought, Fuck that, I ain't got time to run upstairs. I'll have to deal with this here and now.

So I put me right hand in me jacket and walked over to them as menacingly as I could.

'Come on then,' I shouted at the Kosovans. 'Who wants it? Who fucking well wants it? You understand fucking English? You want it? You want it?' I pointed at them individually. 'What about you?'

They all looked scared as shit, and started to step back, as slowly, very slowly, I begin to bring my hand out of my jacket.

I said to Keith, 'Quickly come to me.' And to the girl I shouted, 'Drive off now, love, drive off as fast as you can.'

I was still taunting the Kosovans and they weren't sure what was going on. Then I made a lunge with my hand inside my jacket and they all fled in different directions.

'Thanks a lot for that, Stilks,' said Keith. 'I thought I was really in trouble there. What you got in your jacket?'

'Fuck all, Keith. Remember, I smashed me hand up again recently and I can hardly hold anything in me right hand. You're good at First Aid an' all that, maybe you could have a look at it.'

But don't get me wrong, Sahara's was nothing like Stars. I've never seen anywhere near the amount of trouble there that we had at that place in Greenwich. In fact, Sahara's very much runs itself. A lot of the responsibility is left by the owner in the hands of the doormen and it's policed very well. It's one of the best clubs I've ever worked at, professional from the management down to the bar staff. In fact, it was going so well, and I was working there on Fridays and Saturdays, that another good friend of mine, Jacko, asked me if I'd like to work with him up in the City. He wanted someone who knew the job properly.

'To tell you the truth, Stilks,' he said, 'all we've got is a lot of badged people that have done a doorman's course, but they ain't got no experience. They don't know how to run a door from the front line. Wondered if you could help out.'

So I ask the usual; 'How much?'

We argued about it a bit and then I told Jacko I'd think about it.

I'd known Jacko for quite a while. We used to use the same gyms. I'd go to PecS and Bodywise even after I sold 'em, and we used to hang out together at Reflections in Dartford. I went to them places 'cos I never paid at any of 'em.

I ran into Jacko down at PecS when I called him over and asked if he'd spot for me while I was doin' some bench-pressing. He asked if I'd mind him training with me, and so away we went.

This nice little place he had up in the City was called Minories and was near Tower Bridge. I'd never worked in the City before and I fancied it, but I didn't want Jacko to know that. He was working for a security outfit that looked after quite a lot of places up there.

'Come on, Stilks,' he says. 'It's only one day a week. It's a pub which turns into a club in the evening. You'll love it.'

That's when the light went on in me head. I thought, Right, it's a club, people pay to get in. Right, it's in the financial district. I immediately smelled money and thought it would do me nicely. So I got Jacko to add a few more quid to the money he was offering and that's how I ended up working in the City of London.

It was the usual outfit – dinner jacket and bow-tie. So I got Sheena to sort out the best one I'd got. I didn't want to wear anything that had old blood stains on it for my first day in the City.

I got to the Minories, met the other guys who were working there, all nice lads, and decided to do me usual drill of checking all the fire exits and the rest of it. Seemed OK. I had a good look round and spotted the back door.

'Hey, Jacko,' I said. 'Why's that bloody back door being kept open?'

'Because it's an L-shaped club, isn't it, Stilks. And we need the back door open to keep the air circulating. You'll see later, mate. They can cram the punters in here and it can get terrifically hot. So that door needs to stay open.'

Jacko wasn't fucking joking. When it was packed to capacity, the Minories, which was under an old railway bridge, could hold about 450 people all standing there drinking, elbow to elbow. It used to be heavin', hot and sweaty, and they were all paying £3 a time to get in.

So I said to Jacko, 'If you don't mind, I'll work the back door then.'

'All right, go where you like, Stilks. I'll be down at the front.'

We were supposed to get there at 5.30pm in the evening for a 6.00pm start, but I never got there 'til about 6.15pm. I thought, Bollocks to 5.30, at that time you can't park. After 6.00pm it was all right 'cos you could park on a yellow line. I don't think Jacko ever knew the real reason why I was late all the time.

A couple of weeks went by, I'd sussed out how the place was running, and I'd sussed out where the governor stood. He was by the till and watching that nobody got in for nothing. His wife was behind the bar making sure nobody nicked any money from there and looking after all the credit cards.

The 'suits' from the City would come in and most of them would immediately put their gold credit card behind the bar and get on with the night's drinking. Everyone who deposited their card would be given a number and that's how she kept tally of all the cards behind the bar without getting them mixed up. Champagne was one of the big drinks there. Bottles and bottles of bubbly would be flowing from the moment the suits entered the place. Hundreds of pounds would be going on some of the cards as the night wore on and it got hotter, louder and more packed. They were all getting totally pissed out of their heads.

Soon after I started at the Minories, I met a young lad, Matt Deans, who I decided would be my apprentice. Where I stood at the back door, I couldn't see round the corner, and I didn't fucking well like that but we had all been given little walkie-talkies to keep in touch and they came in very handy. So I said to this kid, who was about 20, 'You are now officially my apprentice.'

And he was more than happy because he had heard all about me, and was pleased to be working with someone who had a bit of a reputation in the game.

So I gave him his spot and told him where to stand, watching the bar, watching the governor and keeping an eye on where Jacko was.

'But, Stilks, ain't I supposed to be watching the punters?' he said.

'You can watch the punters if you like,' I replied. 'But your main job is to watch them three. If his wife comes from behind the bar you get on the mic to me and say, "Is everything all right at the back, Stilks?" Got it?'

'If that's what you want me to do, I'll do it for you.' He was a good lad.

It got to about 7.30–8.00pm and the place was absolutely rammed, all of them standing shoulder-to-shoulder and you can't move in the place. The club policy when you reached that point was one-out, one-in. It was £3 to get in, packed to the fucking rafters and there was a long queue outside.

I'd wait for that queue every week, wait until it was right

round the corner, about 50 people waiting, and then I'd walk to the back of the queue and tap the last person on the shoulder.

'How many of ya?' I'd say.

'Three of us.'

'Right, it's £5 each – this way please.'

'But it's only three quid to get in, mate.'

'Well, it's about an hour-and-a-half wait I guess. But if you want to wait then yeah, it's three quid to get in. You go ahead,' I'd reply. 'But it's £5 this way.'

So they'd all come round the back and give me their fivers. I made them take their coats off first so they looked like they had already been in.

It was all going very nicely. I was nicking the punters off the back of the queue and feeding them into the club through the back door. This went on for a few weeks and then one of the other doormen sussed out what I was doing, so I had to give him some 'hush' money. But that didn't bother me.

Then I got a message over the mic from my apprentice, 'Is everything all right at the back, Stilks?' The governor's missus had moved from behind the bar which meant I mustn't leave my post and go and nick any punters from the back of the queue.

She walked around a bit, checking on where all the doormen were positioned and making sure the security was in place. At the end of the night, if there had been a shout, I would give the apprentice £50 for his pocket. He was a good lad.

The system was working well. This must have gone on for about two months until the governor suddenly started putting two and two together.

Frankly, I was amazed it took him so long to catch on, but it did. The place was more packed than ever by now, and he was taking more money behind the bar than he ever had done. But he knew something didn't add up. He used to use a little hand-held clicking machine which he would click once for every punter that came through the door, so he could keep a tally of how many people were in the club.

The numbers on the clicking machine hadn't gone up, but his takings were sky-rocketing.

'They're getting bloody thirstier and thirstier by the week, this little lot,' he mused once.

'What do you mean?' said his wife.

'Well, we're shifting more champagne and vodka and tonics than we ever have, but the crowd isn't getting much bigger according to my calculations, and the door take is the same.'

'You're joking,' she replied. 'I can hardly get from behind the bar these days. There are lots more people in here than there used to be.'

She was right. The governor still had his 450 punters, but I was letting in another 80 or 100 round the back.

That's when Jacko came up to me, 'The governor says you've got to go, Stilks,' he said. 'Somehow, he's sussed what's going on and he reckons you're the guy behind it. I'm sorry, mate, but he don't want you in here any more. But don't worry, I'll find you somewhere else in the City, you'll be all right.'

'Fuck, Jacko, I liked it up here, I was just getting used to it.'

Now, if I'd been one of them City 'suits' instead of a doorman and been working in one of them fucking big financial institutions, I'd probably have been rewarded for my initiative. After all, everyone had profited from the scheme. The governor was making more money for himself than he had before because of the increase in bar sales; the other doormen and Jacko were getting weighed off to keep shtoom, so they had a bit more money; and the apprentice was getting £50 now and then, so he was happy. And I was paying myself a little extra for showing a bit of initiative. After all, I was working in the financial centre of Europe. But they couldn't fucking see it.

So I thought, What would fuckin' Lenny do, what would Lenny McLean do? I remember when he left Slim Jims, he said, 'The sunbed's mine,' put it under his arm, and took it away with him. That came to mind when I saw these three coffee tables out by the back door. They had marble tops and were worth about £500 each, so I thought they'll do. I got my van and drew up to the back of the Minories. There was another doorman there but I just went past him, picked up one of the coffee tables and started walking back to me van with it.

'Stilks, where ya goin'? What ya doin?' said the doorman.

'What's it look like? I'm taking the coffee tables home.'

'But you can't, you can't do that.'

'Why not?'

''Cos I'm on the back door, they're gonna blame me.'

I said, 'Look, they'd gone before you got here. You didn't see jack shit.'

With that, I put all three tables in the van and drove off down south of the river. I then proceeded to give away the coffee tables to whoever I thought was a deserving cause. One went to an old widow, bless her, who didn't have much to her name.

'Oh, Stilks, that's lovely,' she said. 'You shouldn't have.'

'Don't worry, darling,' I replied, 'it's compliments of the great City of London.'

10

HARD BASTARD

**THAT WHICH DOES NOT KILL US ...
MAKES US STRONGER.**
STILKS

'THE WHAT? WHAT THE FUCK'S IT CALLED?'
'MINSTER PAVEMENT,' SAID JACKO. 'I'VE GOT YOU
A NEW JOB.'

It was another club within walking distance of the
Minories and the head doorman there was a bloke named
Rob Lopez who used to work at the Hippodrome. Black
fella, nice bloke, he showed me round as usual and pointed
out the fire exits and all the time I'm thinking, Where am I
gonna earn a little bit here then?

All the fire exits were alarmed, explained Rob. If you
pushed 'em open, someone has to come to the fire exit to
shut it, because they can only be shut with the right key.
There were all sorts of other security devices around the
place as well.

'Bloody hell, Rob,' I said, 'they take security a bit
seriously here, don't they! Why's that?'

'Because this is the tenth place on the IRA list to be bombed.'

I thought, Fuckin' hell, just my luck.

The security was maximum. There seemed no way I was gonna make an earner out of this one. The IRA were out to blow me up and I couldn't even so much as nick a fuckin' drink.

I thought I wasn't gonna stay inside and get blasted by the music all night so I decided to do the front door with Rob. Again, the governor of this place was always by the till. When any of the punters went out, they were given a pass to show they had already been in once. I was thinkin', There ain't gonna be no drink in this one, but I'd give it a few weeks.

And then I sussed it. On the way out one night, I nicked three or four passes and put 'em in me pocket. When I came to work the next week, I said to Rob I'd show him how to make a few quid. Although he had been a doorman for years, he wasn't that clued up, so I educated him.

As they came to the door, I'd step outside. 'Take your coats off, lads, fiver each, gimme that. Stand to the side.'

Then I'd say to the governor, 'It's all right, they've already been in, they've got the passes.'

But this meant that every week I had to nick a dozen passes just to make a bit of money. I wasn't too happy there, and I told Jacko it wasn't my kind of place. I wasn't making enough money and couldn't figure out any way to do it. After another couple of weeks, Rob got the sack 'cos he was trying to do what I was doin' but he wasn't as good. Poor bloke had been there four years as well.

So Jacko says, 'I know what I'll do. There's a right nice little number, a livener, a right good one and you'll enjoy it. Loads of women. It's the best place we look after and I want you to behave yourself. The reason I haven't given you this one before was because you were too heavy with the punters. But now it might be right for you.'

And that's how I got to go to Bar Med in Old Street in the City.

I phoned the wife up. 'This is it, Sheena,' I said. 'One of the best places in London to be working.'

My job was to make sure no one stood on the stairs. All night long, people were walking up and down the fuckin' stairs but I wasn't to let anyone linger there drinking.

Of course, there's this geezer standing on the stairs.

'Sorry mate, can you get off the stairs,' I say. No reply. 'Off the stairs if you don't mind, sir. It's a very busy area and we must keep it clear.' No reply.

Well, I wasn't going to ask him a third time, so I grabbed hold of him, dragged him up the stairs, pulled him over to where I saw another doorman standing, pushed open the fire exit doors and threw him out.

I was walking back down to my spot when Jacko comes over laughing with this fella I've just thrown out.

I said, 'Jacko, I've just thrown him out.'

'I know, he's just told me.'

'Well, fucking throw him back out then.'

'No, Stilks. You see, he's one of the security guards hired by the company for this place.'

'Well, why didn't someone fucking tell me?' I shouted.

'Don't worry, come up here with me,' said Jacko. So I followed him back up through the club. It was about 8.00pm by now and I had started work at 6.00pm. A small fight kicked off over the back, so Jacko ran over and broke the fight up. He looked at me and pointed at one of the guys as if to say, 'Get rid of that one, Stilks.'

So I grabbed the bloke, and dragged him back to the door while he was shoutin', 'It weren't me, it weren't me.' He was holding on to the door for dear life while I was trying to push him out. So I kick him in the chest and I push him through the door. 'Now stay out,' I say, as he falls backwards and lands on his arse.

Jacko comes over holding some other geezer in a neck lock. 'I didn't mean that one, Stilks,' he says. 'I meant this one,' as he gave the bloke's neck another wrench.

'How was I to know, Jacko? I thought that was the one you was pointing at,' I said.

'Never mind, never mind. Calm down.'

Well, I did calm down until I saw these two girls fighting outside. It was about 8.30pm by now and I'd phoned Sheena to tell her to come up to Bar Med and have a look at what all the fuss was about. I went outside and split up the girls.

'Behave yourself, girls,' I said. 'You go that way and you go that way,' I added, pointing in opposite directions. 'Whatever it is, girls, it ain't worth fighting over.' I went to try and get back in through one of the fire exits but it was closed, which meant I had to walk all the way round to the front to get in. So I walked past a couple of doormen, who were holding the crowd back, and into the lobby. Then the head doorman, Woody, a black fella, elbows me in the ribs. So I stopped and looked round and there was this huge bloke arguing with him. 'If you don't let me in, I'm going to punch your head in,' he was saying. Then he pointed at me and added, 'And I'm going to punch his head in as well.'

So I thought, One thing's for sure, he ain't gonna punch my head in, and with that I hit him straight in the chops. He had a mate who decided to jump in and there we all were fighting in the foyer. I let him have it a couple of times, and then his girlfriend tried to jump on to my back. And as I was shaking her off, by accident I also hit myself in the eye. I'd picked up this little disposable lighter earlier in the night and I'd been clicking it. I still had it in me hand when I hit myself and, of course, I gave myself a black eye, the first ever. Because of all the commotion that was going on in the foyer, someone phoned the police. When the Old Bill arrived, this girl screamed, 'I want him arrested,' pointing at me. 'He's been hitting my boyfriend.'

But with that, I turned to the police and said, 'It's just not true. He's been hitting me. Look, I've got a black fucking eye.'

So we start arguing and it's just at this time that Sheena turns up in a cab outside. She takes one look at me and slowly starts shaking her head.

I'm trying to explain to the police that me and the other doorman have both been attacked, while nursing me black eye. The governor calls me over.

'Listen, Stilks,' he says. 'You can't be hitting these City gentlemen. Here's your money, now go home. And please don't ever come back.'

That was my entire career at the Bar Med. It lasted for three hours from 6.00–9.00pm. I got a black eye, and my full wages.

But I'd loved my time in the City because the punters were not what I expected. I thought that if they were these clever rich geezers, they'd be a bit civilised. But none of it. There was very little difference between them and the blokes down the Plough. After a few drinks – OK, this time it might have been champagne instead of lager – they were all the same animals. I used to look at some of 'em when they were out of their minds or had been in the toilet too long doing lines of Charlie and think, Fuckin' hell, these are the blokes that are running the country's economy. I mean, these pissed-up cunts were working on the Stock Exchange. One of 'em, I remember, was walking round Minster Pavement pinching girls' bottoms, which I thought was unbelievably rude.

'I don't know how you were brought up,' I said to this fucking Hooray Henry. 'But where I come from, we don't tolerate that sort of behaviour. Now stop it.'

But he carried on and so I chased him through the club. He was pushing punters out of the way and spilling drinks and I was right on his tail. Then all of a sudden he goes and hides behind this elderly gentleman. 'The bouncer's going to hit me, the bouncer's going to hit me,' he says in this upper-class accent.'

'I'll do more than fucking that,' I said.

And then the older guy intervened. 'I'm sorry about the lad's behaviour,' he said. 'He's an employee of mine.' I thought, How pathetic, hiding behind the boss.

Although Jacko had lots of clubs up the City, he wouldn't let me near any more of them.

But I just shrugged it off. Who needed a fucking Lord Mayor's Show anyway? I'd got my own little bit of pomp and circumstance at home. My eldest daughter Emma had been made Mayoress of Greenwich and at 14 years old she was the youngest Mayoress in the world.

Don Austen, who had offered me my first job at the Music Machine making sure no harm came to Sid Vicious, also worked with me dad in the butter factory and is a local councillor. Well, he was divorced and his mum was in her eighties. He could have chosen any girl he wanted at the time to be Mayoress, but he asked me if my little Emma would do him the honour of being his escort for the year. I was knocked out by the whole idea. I told him I thought it would be good for her to meet people, and being a Mayoress would be influential on her CV later in life.

We wrote to the *Guinness Book of Records* to tell them she was the youngest-ever Mayoress, but they wanted verification and all that rubbish.

I said, 'It's your bloody book of records, you dig it all out.' They seemed to want everything handed to 'em on a plate.

Anyway, she got the Mayoress's emblem and all that and Don used to take her out about once a month. She got invited all over the place. A limousine would arrive at the house, driven by this geezer named Ernie, and me, Sheena, Don and Emma would go off to all these garden party dos and such like.

In the first month, she went to a march past the Woolwich Artillery in Horse Guards Parade and was taken up to the officer's mess overlooking the ground. She was introduced to all these bigwigs and one of them took a bit of shine to her, I think.

I remember him saying something like, 'And who is that charming young lady over there?'

'That, sir,' said some bleedin' flunky, 'is Miss Emma Stylianou, the new Mayoress of Greenwich. In fact, we believe her to be the youngest Mayoress in the world. She has only just turned 14.'

'Delightful,' replied the bigwig.

It was only later I realised the geezer discussing my daughter was none other than Prince Andrew.

She was also there when Charlton got freedom of the borough which was great 'cos it meant I could go to the football games and sit in the best seats, up there in the restaurant. I met all the players, and had a fabulous time. Most of the people there were just pointing at me going, 'Who the fuck's he?' I didn't give a shit. We had a fantastic time.

When it got to me fortieth birthday party I couldn't find a bleedin' hall to hold it in, so Don says, 'Stilks, 'cos you've been gracious enough to let your daughter escort me as the Mayoress of Greenwich, I'll throw a party for your birthday at the Town Hall.'

All the catering was done, all the drinks, and I invited me close friends and family.

I'd phone 'em up, 'What ya fuckin' doin' Thursday? It's me birthday and I'm holding it in the Mayor's Chamber at Greenwich Town Hall. Come along.'

'How did you manage to swing that one, Stilks?' most of them would say, amazed.

'In this world, it's who you know,' I would say. 'And I happen to know my daughter is Mayoress of Greenwich.'

It was all paid for by the Borough of Greenwich, which I think was put down as some sort of ethnic do. I didn't go mad mind you, it was just a few close friends and family, about 40 people in total.

By this time, I was becoming a bit of a star and getting recognised. 'He's that bloke you don't mess with,' they'd say. 'You know, the doorman bloke.'

Funny enough it was Matt Smith, the young guy who had steamed in when I couldn't hit that fella at Stars 'cos I had a bust hand, that put me in touch with Ronnie Kray's widow, Kate. Me and Matt had become good friends because I'd been trying to give him advice to keep himself out of trouble. But he was always a headstrong young lad, and I knew one day it'd get the better of him.

But on this occasion he came up to me and said, 'Kate Kray is writing a book and she wants me to be in it. I told her it wasn't for me, I didn't want to be in it, but said I had a friend who fitted the description of the kind of fellas she was looking for. Are you interested, Stilks?'

I said, 'What's the fucking book about?'

He goes, 'Well, maybe you'd better meet her first. It's better coming from her.'

In my mind, I'd always had this idea of writing my own book. I'd heard Kate Kray was now a writer and had written a best seller with Roy Shaw and I thought this would give me a chance to talk to her.

So I went along to meet her at a pub in Welling. She was sitting down with her partner Leo. We shook hands, nice people, got down to business.

Kate says, 'I've heard your name mentioned, not just by Matt, but by other people. You're pretty well known and respected in the area and I'm writing a book about 24 different men. I've whittled it down from about 200 and I'm here to see you. If you're the sort of guy I think you are, then I'll put you in the book.

So I said, 'Well, what's the book about, Kate?'

'Hard bastards.'

'Please, Kate, that just ain't me. I'm not a hard bastard, I'm a softie, just ask anyone.'

'I've heard a lot about you, Stilks …'

'Stop it there, Kate,' I said. 'The South East is a big area. I'm not the best fighter in the South East, I'm not the best fighter in Kent, I'm not the best fighter in Bexley. I live in Pennhill Road, it's a fucking long road, Kate, and I doubt if I'm the best fighter in my road.'

She goes, 'Yes, but you've survived more than 20 years on the doors. That makes you a hard bastard.'

There was a short silence, and I said, 'Well, if that makes me a hard bastard, put me in the book.'

And she did. But she also wrote that I had beady eyes and a big nose. I thought, What the fuck's all this? So I asked the wife. 'Sheena,' I said, 'do I really have beady eyes and a big nose?'

'Well, Stellarg, I don't know about the beady eyes but you do have a big nose.'

No one had told me that before and I wasn't having any of it. Three weeks later I got me credit card out, went up to Blackheath Hospital and had me nose done, had it made smaller. It cost me four grand but, after all, it wasn't the bloody National Health Service. The operation took place in the morning and there I was lying in bed waitin' for me mates to come and see me. When they finally turned up there, I had bandages across me face and a plaster on me nose.

I said to one of 'em, 'Come on, you're getting me out of here. You're taking me to work.'

'No, you're fucking mad, Stilks! Don't be so bloody stupid.'

'I ain't mad,' I replied. 'It's Friday night and I ain't stayin' in here. I'm going to work. Look, you go and see if the way's clear and I'll get dressed. You can get me out of here then you can drive me up to the club.'

So I got dressed and sneaked out of my room. As I was walking down, one of the nurses stopped me and asked where I was going.

'Just walking the lads to the front door,' I replied.

As soon as we got there the car was waiting outside so I got in the car and we're off.

I had been at work about two hours with this big plaster across me nose and bandages on my head when these blokes came up the stairs givin' it the big 'un.

One of 'em said to me, 'Look, mate, you've had your nose broken once, you don't want it broken again.' With that I've given him a fuckin' slap and it all kicked off on the staircase over fuck all.

'Now, which one of you wants yours broken as well?' I say. 'How about you?' So he gets clouted and then they're both off out of the club. I managed to get through the rest of the night without any incident and then me mates arrived to take me back to the hospital.

Back there, I hadn't realised that with private health you have personal one-to-one nursing. It's not like a National Health ward where you have one nurse to 3,000 patients. It's a one-to-one thing 'cos you've paid the money. So there's this nurse standing by the door crying.

'What's the matter, love?' I said.

'It's your consultant, he went mad at me.'

'Why'd he do that?'

'Because you were missing. I'd lost my patient. I was supposed to be keeping an eye on you but you gave me the slip. You could have haemorrhaged and died,' she sobbed. 'The consultant says my career could be over.'

I made it back to my room and had a sleep but the next morning the consultant came to see me and he gave me a bollocking as well. But they never found out where I'd been and I never told 'em. I said my mates had just driven me up the road for a coffee.

So when the *Hard Bastards* book was published and it came to the night of the launch at the White Elephant on the River in London, there were big posters on the wall of all the blokes who were in the book. All the papers were there and there were a load of celebrities. I'm standing there with my wife doing me book signing and Kate Kray comes up to me and asks if I'm having a good night.

'Brilliant, Kate, brilliant,' I said. 'Whaddya reckon anyway?

'Reckon about what?'

I said, 'Me nose, what do you reckon about me nose?'

'What about your nose?'

'Look, me nose.' I point at it.

'What?'

'You mentioned that I had a big nose,' I shouted. 'Now look, I've had it done.'

At that Kate burst into laughter. 'You're not telling me you had a nose job just because I mentioned it in the book, are you?'

'Yes I am, and it cost me four fucking grand,' I said exasperated. 'The only thing I've got now that is smaller is me bank balance. And you didn't even fucking notice!'

But anyway, whether it was me new-found good looks or whatever, the next thing I know Kate has been approached about doin' a *Hard Bastards* TV programme and asks if I want to be on it.

I said, 'No, no, that ain't for me. I don't like talking too much and I don't like cameras. I'm not confident enough around 'em.'

Whether or not Kate was having trouble getting the six shows together I don't know, but she started talking me into it. I told her I'd be letting her down but eventually she convinced me to have a go at it.

We started doing the filming and I had gone and fucking well boasted how good I was at judo. We were about half-way through and were doing some shooting up at Sahara's and there was this idiot messing about behind me. So I said to him, 'Get out the way, mate.' But he wanted to be in the shot. 'Out the way,' I repeated. 'We're trying to do some filmin' here.'

With that he got all aggressive and grabbed me, so I ended up hitting him and pushing him down to the floor. One of the other doormen came down while the bloody Mel Gibson wannabe has run off and called the police. Well, that really did it. I'd told Kate I might let her down, but I didn't mean it to be this way. Now everyone was worried that if the guy pressed charges, not only Kate but all the film crew would have to give evidence. So they all decided to disown me for about a month. All they would ever say was, 'Has he pressed charges yet?' But he didn't and so, after a while, they thought it would be all right to resume filming.

'OK, Stilks,' one of the blokes said, 'You've been bragging how good you are at judo, let's see you go through your paces.'

But the fact was, at that time I was a bit rusty. I hadn't been competing for a long time and although I used me Stilks Strangle to silence some of the more unruly fellas in the clubs, I had mainly been using me fists, which explains why some of my knuckles are missing altogether. I had about two weeks to try and get back into shape before they came down the gym to film me.

I thought, Fucking hell! So I put them off for another week to give me a bit of extra time and then phoned up Dave Quin who is one of the best judo experts in the country. He runs a class at the School of Excellence in Dartford, which is one of the finest judo clubs about. We used to train together years ago and so I thought if we could get in three or four workouts a week, I might just be able to pull it off. I had forgotten how hard it was doing judo, especially to get back to a competent level in a just a few weeks. By the time the filming came round, I had split and broken me big toe, dislocated me elbow, was in pain, and had broken my finger. But eventually the film did get made and even now it's shown repeatedly on the Bravo satellite channels. It never turned me into a Vinnie Jones, though.

Hollywood didn't come running to me door; in fact, no fucker did, which was why I had plenty of time on me hands during the week. That's when Jacko phoned me up and said, 'What are you doing tomorrow?'

'It all depends … how much?'

'Eighty quid.'

'For doing what?' I asked.

'I can't tell you, it's secret.'

'Well, that's no good. One, 80 quid ain't enough and two, I wanna know what I'm doin'.'

So Jacko put the phone down and a half-hour later he rings back and goes, 'One hundred and twenty quid.'

I said, 'That's better, but what am I doin'?'

'I still can't tell you.'

'Well, that's no fucking good.'

'All right,' said Jacko. 'But keep it to yourself. We're doing Reggie Kray's funeral.'

'Oh no,' I said. 'Not standing on the road keeping back the crowds.'

'No, Stilks, this is a nice easy one. We are in the cemetery. A handful of top doormen only have been picked to do the cemetery.'

'Why's that?'

'Because they only want the best blokes, who can keep the gangsters out. This is an A-list funeral and we don't want it overrun by C-list villains. Your job is not to keep the public back, but to keep the gangsters out.'

Reggie's widow Roberta insisted that the only people in

the cemetery were close friends and relatives and that rather than former associates in crime, the pallbearers were recent acquaintances, like Tony Mortimer from the pop group East 17. She didn't want it to be like the funerals of Reggie's brothers Ronnie and Charlie and his mum Violet, which were packed with former henchmen and celebrities. Roberta wanted Reggie's passing to be a bit more dignified.

Some of the old-time villains took it as a personal snub and I know Tony Lambrianou, who stayed away, thought it wasn't what Reggie would have wanted at all. But there were floral tributes outside the undertaker's, including roses from actress Barbara Windsor and, although low-key compared with Ronnie's send-off, it was still bloody impressive.

There were 150 security guards in ankle-length navy overcoats with badges and red armbands, to line the route. And the cortège was 18 cars long as it moved from the undertaker's down Vallance Road, where the Kray twins were brought up, to St Matthew's Church. The Victorian hearse was pulled by six black-plumed horses in true East End style and there was a giant crucifix of red and white roses from Roberta.

Apart from Kate, who had married Ronnie, I didn't really know any of the Kray family and I was far too young to have been hangin' around with 'em in their heyday. But I doubt if there was anybody in Britain who had never heard of 'em. Reggie had been banged up for 33 years because of the grip he and Ronnie had kept on the East End of London during the Sixties. But all their gruesome crimes were gangland murders and that's why they had become notorious. They had only been out after their own and that's why there's always been a groundswell of admiration for the brothers in the East End. In the old days, they made sure the streets were safer to walk along and the area safer to live in.

I noticed that the Great Train Robber Bruce Reynolds had made it to the church, as had that bleedin' actor guy Steven Berkoff and even 'Mad' Frankie Fraser. And Roy 'Pretty Boy' Shaw was there as well, if I remember. It had been five years since Reggie's brother Ronnie had died and things had changed, but nevertheless there must have been about 1,500 people gathered outside the church, which I thought well impressive.

Another reason Roberta might have wanted to keep things a bit low-key and less spectacular than Ronnie's parade was because Reggie claimed he had found Christianity after being befriended by a geezer named Ken Stallard, who was a minister for the Evangelical Free Church.

Dr Stallard's words were relayed by loudspeaker to everyone in the churchyard, including me and Jacko.

I could hardly believe it. 'In both Ronnie and Reggie were depths of spiritual feeling which the world never saw or knew,' he said. 'So many people preferred to look at the bad rather than the good.

'There were tears in my eyes when I said to him, "Reggie, do you repent of those things you have done in the past?"

'It was almost as though I should not have asked such a stupid question as he said, "Of course. Of course."'

I thought, Bloody hell, this'll make the papers tomorrow.

Then Stallard claimed Reggie had told him, 'Don't go telling anyone I have become a Christian. That stays until I am gone. I don't want anyone thinking I have done it to get parole.'

Then I remember they played one of my favourite hymns, 'Fight the Good Fight', followed by 'Abide With Me', and 'Morning Has Broken'.

As the coffin was carried from the church by six pallbearers, Jacko turns to me and says, 'OK, Stilks, let's get up to the cemetery straight away.'

'Hold on a fuckin' minute,' I said, 'let's see who else is here.'

In the background, I could hear the strains of 'My Way' by Frank Sinatra which Reggie had requested should be the final song played at the service. And then, following the coffin out of the church, came Bill Murray the actor from the telly series *The Bill* and the former Chelsea footballer David Webb.

Reggie's hearse was adorned with an elaborate wreath that said 'Free At Last'.

'Stilks, are you bloody well coming?' shouted Jacko.

'Hang on.'

It was a nine-mile journey from St Matthew's across London to Chingford Mount Cemetery, and we knew the cortège would take quite a time to get there, so I was in no hurry.

Reggie was to be interred in the same grave as Ronnie

and alongside those of his parents, first wife Frances, and older brother Charlie.

We got to the cemetery in plenty of time and all the security had radio contact with each other. We were told to be on our fucking guard and make sure that only the hearse and the cortège of limousines got in. It didn't matter who they were or how big the face was, if they weren't supposed to be at the graveside, they had to be out. Those were the orders.

That's when we got a message that there were quite a lot of people milling outside the gates of the cemetery and some of 'em were getting shirty with the Ol' Bill. I thought, Fuckin' hell, don't tell me it's gonna go off here.

Some of them were shouting, 'We've got a right to go in, it's a public cemetery,' and all that bollocks.

Jacko goes, 'Right, let's get down there and sort it.'

'Sort who? Who's down there?'

'There's Dave Courtney and his lot, John Daniels and his mates and Charlie Breaker and his mob for starters.'

And I'm thinking, Fuckin' hell, I know them.

'Jacko, I know them blokes,' I said.

'Well, you'd better come then.'

'No, I mean I *know* them. I can't go fucking down there and tell 'em they can't come in.'

'Well, looks like you're going to be the best fella for it. They aren't going to listen to anyone else are they?'

I thought, Fuckin' hell. But I went down there with Jacko and I could see the Old Bill were getting a little worried. They thanked us for coming down there and asked if we could get some of the faces to move out of the way. They were all wearing their black Crombies with their dark glasses on an overcast day. And I thought, Fuckin' hell, talk about dressing up as gangsters!

So I said to 'em, 'Look, lads, don't take it out on me or Jacko, but the wishes of Reggie's wife are that it is close friends and family only.

'Let the cars in and let them do the small graveside service and if you want to show your respects when they come out and have gone, you lot can go in. What about that?'

One or two of 'em started murmuring about it not being fair, so I said, 'Listen, it's a cold day. I'll tell ya what I would do. I would go down the pub and start celebrating from now until they've gone and then come back and pay your respects. Because either way you ain't fucking getting in here at the moment and those are the orders.'

So they all peered at each other through their dark glasses and then they must have decided I was fuckin' Einstein because most of them thought it was a brilliant idea and off they went down the pub.

But Dave Courtney, John Daniels, Charlie Breaker and a few others took Jacko to one side to have a word with him.

That's when he said to me, 'Look, Stilks, do you think we can let this lot in by the other gate. They've promised they'll stand away from the cameras and the relatives and show their respects quietly. They have been friends of the Krays for a long time. Although his wife doesn't want them there, do you think we can get them up there with no trouble?'

I said, 'I don't see why not, as long as they stay right out of the way.'

So we managed to get a couple of faces in and they were out of the way and no one noticed them. But they showed their respects which I thought was a nice thing to do. Dave Courtney, who was a former minder to Charlie Kray, later left a white floral dove with handcuffs round its legs at the gates of the cemetery. 'Gutted', the card read, ''Nuff said'.

While there were thousands of the public outside the cemetery, there were as probably less than 50 at the graveside. It was very dignified, a few words were said and Reggie's coffin was lowered into the grave. As some people picked up handfuls of dirt to throw on to the coffin, I heard a familiar sound. It was a sound that I'd heard many times before. It was a sound that had been with me all my life. Oh no, I thought. Oh no, it can't be. Not bleedin' well here!

But there it was again. Only faintly this time, not like it had been in the sea in Cyprus when I was a kid or when I was on the balcony at Stars. But it was the same unmistakable sound. I thought I must have been going mad, so I decided to walk away from the grave and, as I did, the sound got a little louder. And as I approached the big black limousines, I started to smile.

I said to one of the chauffeurs, 'Hey, mate, do you always keep these big motors ticking over?'

'Yeah, it's best to. If we all started them up at the same time, there would be a right commotion,' he replied. 'It would break the serenity and the calmness of the occasion.

So we usually keep them idling. They're Volvos, and if there's only one or two you can't even hear them. But today there's 16 of them. But they still don't make much of a noise do they? Sounds a bit like those old sewing machines they used to have back in the Sixties. Quite relaxing really. Funny, it's so calm and still at cemeteries that sound is probably the last one to break the silence as a body is laid to rest.

'Anyway, mate, can't stop chatting, here come some of my customers. Got to ferry them back now.'

11

PEN-PALS

**WHEN YOU TALK TO GOD YOU'RE PRAYING,
WHEN HE TALKS TO YOU YOU'RE MAD.**
STILKS

I'D SOLVED THE RIDDLE OF THE FUCKIN' SEWING MACHINE. IT HAD BEEN WARNING ME THAT I WAS GETTING NEAR THE EDGE, GETTING NEAR THE *WHOOSH*! THAT FANTASTIC FEELING, THE FEELING OF EVERYTHING FLASHING BEFORE ME, THE FEELING I ENJOYED, THE FEELING I WOULD DO ALMOST ANYTHING FOR TO EXPERIENCE AGAIN. BUT I NOW REALISED YOU CAN ONLY ESCAPE SO MANY TIMES WHEN YOU'RE TEETERING ON THE EDGE. AND I DIDN'T WANT TO GO THERE ANY MORE. I'D BEEN IN MORE BLOODY SCRAPES THAN I COULD REMEMBER AND I'D SURVIVED THEM. WHAT I AIMED TO DO WAS TO CARRY ON LIVING.

That's when I decided to get in touch with Charlie Bronson. He'd figured in Kate's *Hard Bastards* book, and he was a fucking enigma. So I thought I'd write to him. For me, it was a great honour to be in a book that included Bronson, Roy Shaw, Joey Pyle, Johnny Adair and many of the other notorious villains and gangsters. I didn't think I really fitted into the book but, as Kate said, I had survived many years on the doors and that is a bit of a feat in itself.

I'd been keeping a tab on Charlie Bronson's life through the press and TV for many, many years. Charlie knew about teetering on the edge. He had spent the last 21 years in prisons and asylums. Twenty-four of 'em had been spent in fuckin' solitary confinement, caged up for 23 hours a day. He had been called everything from a lunatic to a serial hostage-taker. Was he mad or was he bad? I didn't fuckin' well know, but I knew one thing – he had been very unfortunate in life. He seemed to me to be the fella who always holds his hand up and says, 'Yeah, I done it. Put me away for it or sentence me in the way you feel fit.' Whereas if I ever did anything wrong, you would have to find me guilty first and prove it. I wouldn't hold me fuckin' hand up to anything. I'm innocent unless anyone knows different.

I read the piece in the book about Charlie and I have always found his sense of humour quite funny and appealing.

Then I read in the papers that he had a son he didn't know about and that he missed seeing him grow up, so I decided to write to him.

Now that's fuckin' weird in itself because I never write to anyone, never. I'd never written to anyone in my life before

Charlie. And it all goes back to my schooldays at Galleon's Mount Infants where I never even learned to read and write. And Bloomfield Secondary School didn't help much either. I wasn't very good at school. School to me was a punishment. Other people seem to look upon it as the best years of their life, but for me it was the worst years and I hated readin' and writin'. I've had very good friends in prison and they have written to me but I never wrote back. Reading and writing used to give me a headache and make me physically ill.

When I wrote to him, I sent him my lucky threepenny piece from 1958. When I was born, me dad had it in his pocket with his change and so he put that in with my birth certificate and all that usual bollocks from when you were a kid. And it has been in that envelope at home ever since. But I thought I'd send me lucky threepenny bit to Charlie because I had been very lucky in life and he had been very unlucky. I told him it was me lucky charm and hoped it would do as well for him as it had done for me.

I wasn't that surprised when he replied because I always thought Charlie was a genuine guy. But I was touched when he started sending me some of his drawings.

And he knew that my wife was having another baby, 'cos it was in the book, so I asked him if he would like me to send him photos of little Nikki, my fifth daughter, and a little progress sheet about how she was growing up. He had never seen his son grow up and I thought he might appreciate it. I would have loved to have him as a godparent for Nikki, but it wasn't possible so I look upon him as a 'godfather from inside'. That's the way I see it.

The first thing Charlie sent was a cartoon he had done called *The Real Elephant Geezer* and a note that read:

I'll get a ring made up of the 3-piece bit.
Kate's up to see me late Feb. I'll give her your best.
Stay tops,
Charlie.

Something just seemed to have clicked between me and him. He probably gets hundreds of letters from all over, but he answered mine and we started getting on OK. He sent me a form from the Home Office so I could visit him, which I had to fill in and send off with three or four photographs. They had to check me out, so I had the CID round asking me mad questions like 'Where did you meet him?' ... 'How do you know him?'... 'When do you want to go and see him?' And this was just to get on his fuckin' visitin' order! I did all that but I haven't gone up to see Charlie yet because I don't want to see him locked up, I don't wanna see him lookin' helpless. When I meet him face-to-face for the first time, I wanna meet him on equal terms on the outside with a glass of something in our hands and toasting our friendship.

Charlie had built up an incredible reputation as a cartoonist, but I didn't realise just how good he was until I started receiving these drawings.

For a man who has been called everything from 'Britain's most feared convict' to a 'brute' and a 'monster' it was interesting to see the real side of Charles Bronson. When he was in Woodhill Prison in Milton Keynes, he was put in a place called Britain's Alcatraz. He has been locked in dungeons in a Hannibal Lecter-type cage, where he was kept naked and fed through a cat-flap, and even in an iron box.

So it came as a bit of a surprise when he sent a note and new cartoon called *Who Said There's No Heaven?* to my little daughter.

He wrote:

Nikki,
Your old dad sent me a photo of you today.
No wonder he's proud of you.
God bless you always,
Charlie.

I regard Charlie as Nikki's surrogate godfather. I'm a religious person and I have had all my kids christened, but it wasn't possible to wait for Charlie to be freed and become her godfather because nobody knows when he's gonna get out. But he's got his own fucking happiness now since he married Saira, although it wasn't bleedin' fair that she had to take a lot of stick in the press over her love for Charlie.

I remember there was one headline that ran WOMAN WHO WANTS TO MARRY A MONSTER. That's really hurtful. But they did eventually get hitched and I remember Charlie making a statement at the time. I kept it 'cos it made me laugh so much.

He wrote, 'I, Charles Bronson, am now saved. Saira Rehman, a beautiful Asian woman, has flown into my life and lit up my dreams.' And then he continued, 'Let me make it 100 per cent clear. I'm on my way to heaven. Me and Saira. (If need be, I'll shoot my way there.) A pump and an Uzi. Ablaze all the way! But I'm going to heaven and if the gates don't open … I'll blow 'em off and I'm going in.'

I think Charlie likes the mad, bad person the press makes him out to be, and he loves to play up to it. But I've seen a softer side of him. I remember once sending him some money and a picture of Nikki. He sent a cartoon and a note back:

What an angel she is! A true beauty. Amazing eyes.
You must be proud. Respect.
I return the photo as it's too precious to keep in this hole.
Photos I rarely ever keep (not in jail).
I've not even got a bed in this place.
Anyway, a lovely beautiful kid. God bless her.
Cheers for the cheque. But I'm sweet. Never worry about
  me.
I'm a man who needs very little.
As long as people treat me Okay … I act Okay.
I basically love the planet … it's just some of the scumbags
  in it that drive me mad.
Kate is up 28th to see me. We always have a laugh.

He invited me to his wedding up at the Manhattan Cafe in Woolwich which I went to, although, of course, not to the actual ceremony. There were lots of his close friends there, good people like Dave Courtney, Tony Lambrianou, Joey Pyle and Vic Dark. We all drank to his good health and we made a video of all of us wishing him all the best for the future. And then we sent it to him and he watched it.

I didn't really know what to buy Saira and Charlie for the wedding, so I put a cheque in an envelope, but several weeks after the wedding I noticed that the cheque hadn't been cashed. I thought, Oh no, not fuckin' again. What's the matter with these people, don't they like money? I asked Kate why they hadn't cashed the cheque and she phoned Saira. They'd had so many cards and, while going through them, the cheque must have got mislaid or thrown away. In the end, I got Saira to give me her bank details and put the wedding gift straight into her account.

There was a lot of fuckin' nonsense written about that wedding and their marriage. The worst one was a story in the *People* claiming that Charlie was demanding a divorce after only 18 days of marriage. It was a complete load of bollocks.

It said Charlie accused Saira of 'unreasonable behaviour' and then went on to quote some 'prison insider', which must have been made up, saying, 'Charlie is boiling with rage. His marriage has not worked out at all like he thought it would.' That was completely untrue.

And then it went on, 'He's been in solitary confinement

for 23 years and having a commitment is too much ... He threatened to attack 12 officers in the exercise yard; screamed abuse as guards in riot gear arrived at his cell; and demanded that divorce papers be sent to him.'

At the time, the bleedin' authorities had decided to move Charlie from Woodhill Prison to a special wing in Wakefield Prison and put him back in the cage. If anything was guaranteed to get him mad it was that, but it wasn't anything to do with Saira or his love for her.

And I know because I got a note from him soon after he arrived in Wakefield thanking me for the wedding gift. In it, he absolutely denies any idea of divorce and restates his love for Saira and Sami.

Here's the full text and the strange cartoon he sent with it. I want people to read this and know the truth.

Charlie wrote:

Very kind of you to send 'gift' to Saira (meant a lot to me).
A lot of lies in the media over our lives.
Sick people, sucking and chewing off my name.
Sell their soul (cat away, mice play).
Take it from me, my love for Saira and Sami is my life.
Prison has never changed me in 30 years.
Saira done it in 30 seconds.
My respects
Charlie.
P.S. The only divorce for me is my crime days. Believe it!
Back up in the cage.

Although Charlie has never seen me in person, he has seen photos and videos of me that were sent to him from the wedding reception we held, and from the *Hard Bastards* book launch. And from that he drew another cartoon of me and him which I really cherish. I remember writing back to him sayin', 'Charlie, that portrait of me and you together is better than a photograph,' and I told him I was gonna use it in the book.

He wrote back saying:

Blimey, it wasn't that good a portrait.
(I can do better) but I've got to be in the right mood
(I'm a cartoonist see).
But I'm pleased you like it.

Then he mentions the fact his appeal would be up shortly and adds:

I've got to get this life squashed
And get the fuck out of these asylums.
They're all raving mad
And that's just the screws.
P.S. But I've got my wonderful wife and daughter (So I've
  got the world).

I think Charlie is someone who is really misunderstood, he's game for a laugh, but he seems to hold his hands up for anything and everything. He won't let anybody take the piss. Whereas sometimes you should shut your mouth a little bit and live to fight another day, with Charlie he wants to have it out there and then. I think he should be given another chance, because there are a lot of people in jail who have done a lot worse crimes than he has. They've all been given second chances and fucked off, whereas he has never been given a chance.

Charlie has a charity he supports. He gives a lot of the money he gets from the auctions of his pictures and one thing and another to Help a London Child, and some time this year I am going to do a walk for him to help his charity. He's a very humane bloke and thinks about other people before he thinks about himself. I honestly think he is misunderstood and there is a soft side to Charlie that people don't know.

But in Britain, the media likes to make out that some hard bastards in jail are really evil monsters. But that ain't always true. The really evil cunts are the paedophiles and the serial sex killers. OK, Charlie might have done some armed robbery in his time, and he's held his hand up for it. But when it comes down to real violence, he has only dished it out to people who deserve it.

Sometimes, you can see the deep hurt inside Charlie from the drawings he sends to me. You can see that hurt and you can understand it because this geezer has been in the worst forms of solitary confinement for more than a couple of decades. It's not easy to rise above all that crap, so no wonder his latest book is called *Insanity*.

I told Charlie I was thinking of writing me autobiography and that it weren't all gonna be made up like so many of these so-called villains' books you read. I told him I didn't care how humble my story was – after all I'm only a doorman – at least it was gonna be for real. None of this fucking bollocks about going to America and cleaning up the bleedin' Mafia and all that shit from someone who's never been outside the fucking M25.

And he wrote back to me with encouragement and understanding.

He wrote:

A book, remember, is for life
It lives on.
It can hurt some, destroy others
Enlighten others
Stick to the facts, and if it hurts
Fuck 'em.

12

HARD ... AS EVER

**I NEVER FORGET A FACE,
BUT AS THE OLD BILL KNOW
I CAN NEVER REMEMBER A NAME.**
STILKS

THEY CIRCLE EACH OTHER AND *BANG!* IN GOES THE LEFT PAW. THEY'RE FUCKIN' SPITTIN' AT ONE ANOTHER.

'Scram!' I shouted at the two cats fighting on the patio. 'Get the fuck out of here.'

I was trying to concentrate on me latest little earner. I was still working the weekends up at Sahara's and that was going OK, but I kept finding meself at a loose end.

I'd sold Bodywise and was indoors not doin' a lot, just gettin' under the wife's feet. She was getting the hump and I was getting restless, but above all I didn't really have many 'pennies' of me own to spend as I pleased. I was always asking the wife for £15 or £20 a day to go up the caff, get a bit of petrol, that sort of thing.

That's when Little Dave knocks on the door this time.

That's Dave Joy who used to work for me at Bodywise and I hadn't seen him for six months.

'How are you, Dave? I said.

'Not too good. I haven't worked since I worked for you,' he replied.

'Oh fuckin' hell. I haven't been doin' a lot either.'

So we were chattin' away when all of sudden Dave says, 'I've got this idea.'

'What's the idea, Dave?'

He goes, 'I used to do a bit of banger racing and I know about tyres.'

'What do you know about tyres?'

'Well, I know the sizes.'

There was a bit of a pause and so I looked at him straight and said, 'Blimey, Dave, you know a bit more than me. So what are you saying?'

'Well, there's money in tyres.'

So I thought, Right. My Gumbarro, Greek Mick, had a shop down in Crayford which was empty. I got in touch with Mick and he said we could use the shop. The next thing I had to do was go to the bank and see if I could borrow ten grand to buy the equipment for running a tyre shop.

I made an appointment, went up to the Nat West, and had a word with the manager.

'I need ten grand to open a tyre shop,' I told him.

'Well, have you brought a business plan I can see?'

'No.'

'Well, you'll need a business plan,' he laughed slyly. 'We'll have to see a business plan.'

'Listen, mate, I've been with you since I was 19 years old.'

'But you still need a business plan,' he insisted.

'Look here. If I knew how to read, write and do fuckin' business plans I'd be working nine to five up in the city, not fucking asking you for money to start me own business.'

He had really pissed me off so I picked up the chair and threw it at him and walked out.

Then I went to Barclays Bank, the Woolwich, Lloyds TSB, the lot. And none of them would give me a fucking loan because I had never had any business with them. All me mortgage and paperwork and everything else had been sorted for me by the Nat West. The wife didn't like the idea of me putting up the house for security, so I somehow had to get a personal loan, which meant I had to go back to the Nat West and face them again.

But this time I decided bollocks to the local bloke, and instead I phoned the Area Manager and told him that the bank manager didn't understand me and wanted to see business plans and all that.

Anyway, the Area Manager, a bloke named Tony Mundon, agreed to see me. He asked me what I wanted the money for and I told him straight – 'Tyres'. We talked for five or ten minutes about the new shop and then he said he'd come down and have a look at it.

He wanted to know what we were going to spend the money on, and I explained we were buying machines and one thing and another. It got tricky when he asked how much profit we thought we were going to make because me and Dave didn't even know where we were going to buy the tyres from yet never mind how much profit. So I did my normal stuff and bullshitted him and then he said the magic words, 'All right, I'll put the money in your account this afternoon.'

And that's the way you have to do it if you want things to work out. The local bank manager only wants a business plan so he can show it to the Area Manager anyway and cover his own back. If you can cut out the local man, you can cut out a lot of the shit.

We managed to open the shop and everything was going smoothly. We were just dealing in car tyres and alloy wheels. It was all going really well. I'd financed it and Dave was looking after the shop and we split the profits 50-50. If we made £100 he would get £50, and if we earned nothing he'd get half of that as well.

Dave was working hard one day and this fella came in and made up some story about someone catching a cab from the shop and not paying the fare, which came to a staggering £160. It was all a load of bollocks and Dave told him he didn't know anything about it.

So the bloke shouts at Dave, 'Look, you owe me £160 and I want it.'

'Do me a favour, mate,' says Dave. 'No one here owes you fuck all now piss off.'

With that, the bloke grabs a hammer and starts jabbing it into Dave's face.

'If you don't gimme the money, I'm gonna smash this hammer over your head,' he shouts like some fucking loony. So Dave, being cautious, goes into his pocket and takes out all his cash which is about £100, and gives it to him. The bloke goes, 'Right, mate, I'll be back tomorrow for the rest, and if you haven't got it I'm going to pour petrol over you and set you on fire.'

So Dave's phoned me up. 'Stilks,' he says. 'Some fucking lunatic has just come in and robbed the shop and says he'll be back tomorrow for more.'

'Whaddya mean robbed the shop?'

'I had to give him £100, Stilks.'

'You did fucking what?' I exploded.

'I had to, he was waving a hammer at me.'

'I don't fucking care.'

'Don't have a go at me, Stilks. You'd have cared if he had hit me over the head with the hammer.'

'If he'd done that, I'd still have had a go at you – for not giving him the money.'

Dave couldn't win. But the next day, I decided to accompany him to the shop when he opened up in the morning. At about 10.00am, I was round the caff getting something to eat when Colin Miller, my second pair of eyes and ears, comes running in shouting, 'He's back, he's back.'

So I left me breakfast and started winding meself up, getting well fucking psyched for this one. 'I'm gonna do him, I'm gonna do him,' I kept repeating over and over to myself. Then I blasted into the shop, saw this guy and *bang*! I hit him once, then another, and one into his chest.

I threw him up against the wall, and then a thought occurred to me and I said, 'Dave, is this the one?'

The shop was full of customers and I just picked on the biggest and ugliest one. 'Dave, is this the one?'

Dave goes, 'Yes, that's him.'

I thought, Thank God for that, and gave him one in the face. There was a bit of a struggle 'cos he was a fucking big fella, but I managed to get him in a headlock. I put another one in his face. I was hitting him but he bloody well wasn't going down. Fuck it, I hit him again.

By this time, Dave had phoned the Old Bill but before they arrived, a mate of mine named Craig turned up, opened the door and saw me hitting this bloke with his head down.

'Ahhh, just what I want,' said Craig, and he kicked the geezer straight in the head.

Then Max, who'd worked with me at the Station and who I hadn't seen for about three years, walks in and gives the bloke another kick.

I pushed Craig and Max away. 'Leave him alone,' I shouted. 'Let me do him.'

I grabbed the guy and lifted him up. 'So you wanna rob the shop do ya? Let's have it, you and me, a straight'ner.' So I'm hitting him, he's bleeding, I've got him in another headlock. I'm giving it 100 per cent and trying to put him out, but he won't go. I hit him in the face and half a tooth breaks off. Later, I looked all over the floor for it because I thought it would be nice to have it made into a ring.

And just at that moment, the Old Bill walked in. For a minute, I wondered if they were going to give him a kick as well. I immediately dropped the bloke and went to walk out of the shop.

'Oi, where do you think you're going?' said one of the police.

'I'm leaving, mate, I'm a customer. I don't want to get involved in any of this. This is nothing to do with me.'

As they parted to let me out, I heard one of them ask the fella what had been going on.

'Nothing,' he replied. 'I came in like this.'

But the Old Bill recognised him and the last I saw he was being bundled into the back of the police car. Later, Dave got a call from the police who said, 'I bet you won't be pressing charges, will you?'

'No, I don't think we will,' said Dave very politely.

The next day an envelope came through the door of the shop – and in it was £100! Not bad, I was about to take the kids on holiday.

I like to think of meself as a controlled gambler. I don't lose money that I can't afford. I don't lose me shopping money or the baby's nappy money. But I'd got the spending money together for us to go on holiday and I thought, Wouldn't it be nice if I could go in the betting office, double the spending money, and then we'd have a bit more.

I knew it was a stupid idea but I felt myself being dragged towards the fucking betting office. I thought, OK, I'll just bet half the spending money. Of course, I lost. So I decided I wouldn't go home, instead I'd go down the dog track. I went down the dogs and that's where I done in the other half of the spending money.

Oh no, not again, I thought. What the fuck am I gonna tell Sheena? Now I was in trouble. This was on the Thursday night and we were supposed to be going on holiday the following Tuesday. There was only one thing for it. I would have to go and see Paul Thomsett the dog trainer I'd known since I'd bought Capital Cinema all them years ago.

'Paul, Paul,' I said, 'I've fucking done all me money in.' Paul was a good friend of mine by now and, normally, if I had a little win he would drag me away from the dogs and tell me to go home.

'What's the matter this time, Stilks?' Paul replied.

'I've gambled away all the kids' holiday money and I don't know what to do.'

He told me to come up to his farm on Sunday because he had a lot of good dogs that would be running on Monday night.

'But I haven't got any fucking money,' I explained, 'I can't bet on anything.'

'Just come up the farm on Sunday.'

So I went up there and he told me that all his dogs were fit, they were all running well and they were all in with a chance the next day. So he wrote down a list of six dogs and told me to go and do an Alpha bet with the six of them. It's a combination bet on all the dogs. 'Do that, Stilks, and I'm sure you'll get your holiday money.'

'But I ain't got no money for the bet,' I say.

'Fucking hell, Stilks, how much have I got to do for you? Here, have £200 as well and just make sure that I get me money back and give me a drink.'

So I went down the betting office and put the money on. Then on the Monday I saw Paul to reassure myself the dogs were still fit and well. They were. Everything was set. Now all we could do was sit back and watch the racing, with fingers crossed.

The first one wins.

The second one wins.

The third one is a photo finish. 'Fucking hell, Paul, it's lost, it's lost,' I cried.

'Hold your nerve, Stilks, hold your nerve.'

It's judged to be the winner.

The fourth one is in.

Fifth and sixth – all in. Six bloody winners!

I'm jumping up and down celebrating, the winnings would come to many thousands of pounds. 'I've done it, Paul, I've done it,' I yelled.

'Oi you,' he said. 'Don't you go fucking missing. You owe me my drink.'

What a diamond geezer. Not only had he got me out of trouble, but the holiday spending money had been replaced, the holiday had also been paid for and I bought myself a car.

By this time, the *Hard Bastards* book had already become a bestseller and I was getting recognised in and around Crayford with people saying, 'I know you, you're that Stilks fella, ain'tcha?' And when the TV programme was shown, even more people started recognising me. 'Oi, haven't I seen you on the telly, mate?' some would say.

Once, the police stopped me for not having a tax disc on me car. And when they asked for my particulars, I gave them the usual, a name and address and date of birth of someone I'd known years ago at school. I always use that one. But as I was getting ready to drive off, promising to go to the station later with verification of who I was, a young copper came up and joined his mates. He took one look at me and said, 'Hey, didn't I see you on the telly last night?'

'Nah,' I said. 'Don't know what you're talking about officer. I ain't never been on the telly. Anyway, I'm in a hurry.' And with that I put me foot down and I was off.

I'd had to get myself in shape very quickly for the TV programme and I was determined to keep myself in shape by working out regularly. So me and my training partner Dennis Supple started going up the David Lloyd gym where I didn't really know anybody, but it was OK 'cos we could do our training without anyone yelling 'seen you on the telly' or any of that shit.

When it comes to training, I like to do what I want to do. I like the person with me to follow me, I don't like to do someone else's workout. So Dennis agreed he'd come and train with me. We'd been training together for years.

I was up there training one day and this big fucking lump walks over, and I don't recognise him. I'm on the bench pressing a few weights and he says, 'Hello Stilks.'

I just go, 'Hello mate.'

'Don't you recognise me?'

'Nah, sorry, mate.'

'Pete Robinson.'

And then I look up properly. 'Bloody hell, Pete, I ain't seen you for fucking years. You've put a bit of weight on.'

I'd known Pete 'cos he worked the doors as well. I'd met him on the circuit. Last I knew he was down the Station in Gravesend.

He says, 'Yeah, I've been taking steroids, building myself up, I like looking big. Mind you, you ain't very strong are you, Stilksy?'

'Nah, Pete, I've got a few injuries at the moment.'

'I'm probably quite a lot stronger than you.'

'Are you, Pete? That's good, mate. Anyway, excuse me, I've got to carry on.'

So he goes and does his workout, and Dennis is doing a bit of spotting for me and I take no notice of what was said.

A couple of days later, we go up to the David Lloyd again and there's Pete Robinson, so I give him a bit of a wave, just to be friendly. Me and Dennis are training and over comes Pete again.

'Yeah, Stilks, I'm doing a lot of boxing at the moment.'

'Nice, Pete, good one. Well done.'

'Yeah, I can take out that black mate of yours Dave Stewart now, easy, easy.'

'That's good. Well done,' I reply and get back to my workout.

'Yeah, I've got a fucking strong right hand.'

'That's lovely.' I'm thinking, This bloke is getting on my fucking tits. But anyway, he goes away and we all go back to our routines. This was all around last Christmas time, coming up to New Year.

Then he comes over again. 'I hear you're at that old people's place, Sahara's, now, ain't you, Stilks? Where I work it's a lot harder than your place.'

'Yeah, you're probably right, Pete. Listen, mate, I don't want to be rude, but I've come here to get on with me trainin' if you don't mind.'

He goes, 'Yeah, I'm on £90 New Year.'

I thought, Fucking muppet. I wouldn't even go to work for fucking £90 a night. But I didn't want to get into a conversation or have an argument with him, so I said, 'Fucking brilliant, that's well done.' He was working at a place much harder than mine and he was doing it for £90. Brilliant.

Me and Dennis go up the David Lloyd another night and what should fuckin' happen but this fucking idiot comes over again.

This time it's, 'I've always been better looking than you, ain't I, Stilks?'

I'm thinking, OK, OK, just one more.

'What you doing up here training anyway?'

'I've just done a TV programme for that *Hard Bastards* book I was featured in and I want to stay in shape, if you'll just fucking let me. All you've been doin' is disturbing me workouts, Pete.'

'What the fuck was you doing in that book in the first place anyway? I should have been in that book.'

Well, that did it. I thought it was an honour to be in that book with guys like Charlie Bronson, Roy Shaw and John McGuinnes. So I said, 'Whaddya mean I shouldn't have been in that book?'

'Well, all those other people have got a lot of history.'

'Well, I've been on the doors 25 years, Pete. What are you trying to say?'

'You're fuck all, Stilksy, I'm bigger than you and I should have been in the book.'

'Oh I see,' I said with a little nod. 'I see now. Right then, anyway, I got to go.'

And with that me and Dennis went and got changed. I told Dennis roughly the whole story and added, 'Den, I think he's taking the piss out of me. Whaddya think?'

Dennis goes, 'I suppose so.'

'In which case, I'll tell ya what I'm fucking well gonna do, Dennis. There are two people I want to bash up and I'm going to make it my New Year's Resolution to bash up Pete Robinson and this other geezer who's been getting' on my nerves. That's my New Year's Resolution. And I want you to do me a favour. If you ever see me having a fight with someone, don't grab hold of me and try and stop me because you'll be giving the advantage to the other fella. Do me a favour, if you think you wanna stop the fight, grab hold of the other fella. Not me.'

I had got it firmly in my mind that I was gonna do Pete

Robinson and knew if Dennis was around he would try and stop me.

New Year's Day came round and me and Dennis decided we would train really hard from the first day of the year and get totally fit. So off we went up to David Lloyd's, up the stairs, open the door, and the first person I saw was Pete Robinson.

I went, 'Happy New Year, Pete, I want a word with you.'

'What's that about?'

Bang! He's gone straight down.

'What's up, what's up?' he shouts

'Fucking better looking than me, you cunt.' And I started kicking him in the head. But he manages to struggle up and he's got me in a vice-like grip. I manage to break free and *bang*! another solid hit and he goes right over one of the benches.

'I don't want to spoil your fucking good looks,' I scream. 'But I'm going to,' and I land a beautifully pitched left. He reaches out to pick up one of the weights, one of the dumb-bells. I see him going for it and I smash a thunderous blow into his arm. He can't pick fuck all up now! I rain a few blows down on his head. But he's a strong cunt and he catches me with one on my right shoulder. I hit him back with a real stinger. A cut over his eye starts to open up and blood is pouring down his face. I knew then that I'd got to knock him over once and for all.

I'm kicking him round the gym shouting, 'You're nothing but a fucking muppet, Pete, a fucking muppet. You ain't better lookin' than me now, you fuckin' muppet.'

He manages to blurt out, 'Nah, you've got the wrong idea, Stilks, I never meant it like that.'

But it was too late.

There was blood all over the David Lloyd gym. All the other people in the place had fled while the fight was going on and the manager of the place came up the stairs and went straight over to Dennis.

'Are you all right?' he asked him.

'Yeah, 'course I am,' said Dennis. 'But *he* ain't over there,' pointing to Pete Robinson who's eye had now really opened up.

He ran over to Pete. 'What's happened, what's happened?'

'Nothing, I just fell over,' he managed to gurgle.

'Oh, all right then, I'll go and get the accident book.'

Pete turned to me and said, 'I saved you there, Stilks, you owe me one.'

'Owe you one, do I, owe you one? Yes, I suppose I do you one.'

And once again I was up there, I was in the middle of it …. And very slowly, very slowly I started to wind one back, all the way back. I was tensed and flexed and I was about to deliver the ultimate straight'ner. I held Pete at arm's length and then whispered to him, 'Do you wanna know the real reason I'm a hard bastard?' Then I let it go with as much force as I'd ever let one fly in my life.

Bang!

ACKN⊕WLEDGEMENTS

I would like to thank all these doormen for looking after me for all these years. I wouldn't be here today without them. If I have forgotten anyone, then I apologise; my thanks go to you to...

Tony Lee – Hard Bastard; Brad Sharpe – fearsome; Peter Davies – strongest man I know; Donald Austin – The Mayor; Leon – always there; Matt Summers – knows how to pull a sort; Reg Parker – The Organiser; Johnny Madden – The Ultimate Pro; Baz Allen – The Enforcer; Dave Bowdry – best right hand in the business; Little Jim – Crooklog gym; Charlie Glencross – fearless; Tony Denim – diplomat; Jimmy Hayes – old school; Roy King – always there; Little George – Mr T; Craig Wybrow – loophole; Andy CD – upfront; Jacko – fucking frightening; Cass Pennant – ICF; Bob Leonard – old school; Seamus Wall – never let you down; Geoff Frowd – mad eyes; Ray Grey – good head doorman; Mick Wilson – good roundhouse; Danny Wilson – good athlete; Kev Harrison – gets on with it; Lawrence Powell – loves a motor; Lee Halford – The Grappler; Nick Netley – not to be trifled with; Mark Parish – powerful bible-basher; Dave York – Man Mountain; Roy York – the referee; Terry Coombs – gentleman; Dave Stewart – knows how to box; Tony Ward – pick the bones out of that!; Kevin Wishart – watch his head; Peter Hayford – Penguin; Nicky Green – big bencher; Dave Hold – smooth talker; Lindon Pursey – fucking tall; Max Jacobs – no fear; Jack Jacobs – keep clear; Joe Walker – growler; Dave Kilroy – loves a Fosters; Michael Bredo – good doorman; Terry Rich Jnr – short fuse; Jimmy Barthweight – big hands; Bill Gough – sexual athlete; Para Bob – athlete; Gary Brown – bulldog; Andy Henry – good head doorman; Micky Filbert – dangerous; Keith Price – always prepared for the worst; Paul Macky – loves a computer; Wayne – dapper; Lloyd – Elle McPherson's bodyguard; Les – head of the ice rink; Steve Chamberlain – Mr Judo; Kelly Stepons – The Post; Kevin Eagen – The Colonel; Danny Webb – loves his gold; Tony Ash – one more rep; Chris Holly – serve em up; Peter Ambrigiou – The Squaddie; Bill Marney – Brains; Terry Kilroy – The Wrestler; John McGinnis – disturb at your peril; Matt Smith – absolute lunatic; Horice Notice – Champ; Baz – one of the best; Chris – The Cosh; Irish Tom – The Irish; Gypsy Tom – loved it; Archie – tremendous fighter; Martin Smith – bulletproof; Dennis and Tony – good black guys; George Hayes – powerhouse; Clayton – loved it; Big John – can use both hands; Dutchy Peter – The Regulator; Peter No Legs – big; Sid Brown – The Negotiator; Glenn Dwyer – smooth operator; Glenn Hammond – always starts them; Tony Wedge – young and up and coming; Ken – big man; Matt Deans – The Apprentice; Mark Deans – STRANGE!; Rob Lopez – no problem; Jamie – knows his way around a club; Gordon – flash; Woody – city gentleman; Micky Stevens – The Shadow; Kim York – Man Mountain's brother; Mick – Bebas Mick; Chris Plender-Lieth – The Giant; Gary Fox – The Paramedic; Carlo Scott – deep voice; Eddie Cooper – powerful; Mark Rowe – The Trainer

Thanks to all my family and friends for being there when I needed them:

Peter Doyle, Derek Lavierre, Peter Matkins, Tom and Tia, Dougie, Jeff Batteridge (RIP), Keith Brown, Gerry Levelle, Ricky Emmings, Lenny Powel, Roger Powel, George Powel, Danny Boon, Johno Boon, Wayne Stewart, Les Stewart, Stewart Smith, Trevor Smith, Scott Wilson, Gary Wilson, Gary G, Martin John (RIP), Keith Deals (RIP), Sanjay Ravel, Tony Gorga, Paul Johnson, Terry Corriley, Darrel Anderson, Brian Coville, Chris Cummings, Peter Lett, Dave Arnold, John Maggot, Huey, Jack Shepherd (RIP), Rob Sondhi, Loudemair, Mich Levelle, Chriss (Saharas), Kevin Groombridge, Steve Groombridge, Steve Mason, Mick Calcott, Jeff Moore, James Moore, James Calcott, George Brown, Mark Goldwin, Dave Welch, Karen Simms, Kerry Player, Pierre Lavierre, Dave Quinn, Kevin McKay, Gary Robinson, Eric Cox, Alan Cox (RIP), Keith Waghorn, Baines, Strombrowski family, Mick (tattoos) Terry Kilroy, Keith Bloomfield, Jean, Alex Constantine (RIP), Dennis Supple Snr, Bob (Saharas), Mark Rowe, Rob Davies, Jeff (Judo), Dave Chandler, Nick Smith, Michael Ross, Chriss Reece, Bob Tomlin, John Selby, Steve Selby Mike Collins, Mike Parker, Dennis Supple, Marco Puzio, Allan Pilkington, Alex and Danny, Big Reg, Mark Wheeler, Mark Galimore, Neil O'Shawnesy, Colin Miller, Dave Joy, Jamie Budgen, Tony Langley, Johnny Lynch, Gary Smail, Gary Cross, Lou Payne, Nicky Payne, Martin Payne, Ray Parker, Micky Taylor, John Taylor, Maynard Rooms (RIP), Trevor Rooms (RIP), Mark Rooms, Gunter Rooms, Terry Rooms, Kate Kray, Leo O'Riley, Gary Fox, Steve Ward, Noel Healy, Rob Davies, Paul Docherty, Peter Lane, Andy Callard, Diane How, Paul Clark, Gary Brightwell, Keith Goddard, Pat Gavin, Charlie Bronson, Charlie Braker, Julius Francis, Kevin Gillespie, Steve Mournders, Derek Marshall, Jeff Whitlow, Dave Tag, Erica Wedge, Steve Albon, Ron Weatherly, Matt Grey, Terry Rich, Billy Marney, Harry Marney, Michael Williams, John Cole, Frank Melbourne, Dave Enfield, Ian Tucker, Mark Watts, Keith Gladis, Barry Bartholemew, Ricky Bonner, Geoff Bettridge (RIP)

The Greeks

Bishop Christopher, Mick Peters, Andrew Michael, Max Jacobs, Jack Jacobs, Tony Papa-Adams, George Georgiou, Andrew Lucka, Tony Panai, Panai Galanis, Yanai Ianou, Tony Lambrianou, Andy Costi, George Costi, Con Costi, Angelo Costi, Dino Orphanou, Panicos Panayi, Andy Ilsden, Charlie, Naz, Dennis Ibrahim, Iaden Ibrahim, Adam Papa-Adams, Chris Kyriacou, John Everett, Andrew Gallimore

If anyone wants to get in touch with Stilks for consultancies or general enquiries on security matters, you can do so at:
Crayford Tyres, 4 The Parade, Crayford Way, Kent, DA1